Rover 3½ Litre Owner's Maintenance Manual

Incorporating: Saloon and Coupé models

The Rover Company Limited
Solihull, Warwickshire, England

Factory Service Department
Solihull, Warwickshire
Telephone: 021-743 4242
Telegrams: Rovrepair, Solihull
Telex: 338541

London Service Department
Seagrave Road, Fulham, London SW6
Telephones:
  Administration and Appointments: 01-385 1221
  Reception: 01-385 7721
  Parts Department: 01-385 6231
Telegrams: Rovrepair, Wesphone, London

Specification details set out in this handbook apply to a range of vehicles and not to any particular vehicle. For the specification of any particular vehicle owners should consult their Distributor or Dealer.

The Manufacturers reserve the right to vary their specifications with or without notice, and at such times and in such manner as they think fit. Major as well as minor changes may be involved in accordance with the Manufacturer's policy of constant product improvement.

Whilst every effort is made to ensure the accuracy of the particulars contained in this Handbook, neither the Manufacturer nor the Distributor or Dealer by whom this Handbook is supplied, shall in any circumstances be held liable for any inaccuracy or the consequences thereof.

By Appointment to
Her Majesty
Queen Elizabeth II

Manufacturers
of Motor Cars and
Land-Rovers

By Appointment to
Her Majesty
Queen Elizabeth
the Queen Mother

Suppliers
of
Motor Cars and
Land-Rovers

English Version Part No. 605215

Rover 3½-Litre

H893

Introduction . . . .

This book has been prepared to provide supplementary information to that contained in the Owner's Instruction book. Its intention is to give clear and simple information necessary for the efficient care and maintenance of your car.

The book is divided into four sections:

Part 1   Routine maintenance and adjustments.
Part 2   Electrical equipment, body work, etc.
Part 3   General data and index to Parts 1 and 2.
Part 4   Free Service and Maintenance Schedules.

The new car pre-delivery check will have been carried out by the Distributor or Dealer responsible for the sale of the car, leaving a stub in the book to certify that the work has been done.

The routine maintenance of this car has been kept down to a minimum and can, if desired, be carried out by owners without special tools. Any work beyond that detailed in this book should be entrusted to Rover Distributors or Dealers who are equipped and prepared also to carry out the routine maintenance.

It should be noted that the sequence of normal maintenance repeats itself every 32.000 km (20,000 miles).

The Rover Company is always prepared to give advice on maintenance or other matters to individual owners, but any correspondence with the Company *must bear the chassis or car number* which will be found on a plate affixed to the left-hand front door pillar.

PART ONE

ROUTINE MAINTENANCE AND ADJUSTMENTS

Notes on general maintenance

Lubrication and maintenance are necessary to keep any car in good mechanical condition. All the items which require regular maintenance as detailed in the Maintenance Section are shown in Part One of this book in terms of mileage which would apply in a temperate climate. Climatic and operating conditions affect maintenance intervals to a large extent; in many cases, therefore, the determination of such intervals must be left to the good judgment of the owner or to advice from a Rover Distributor or Dealer, but the recommendations will serve as a firm basis for maintenance work.

Of particular importance in this connection are the undermentioned items:

IMPORTANT

1 Every 1.000 km (750 miles) check engine oil level, power steering oil level and water level in radiator and windscreen washer reservoir.

2 Drain and refill engine sump and change the oil filter every 8.000 km (5,000 miles) or every six months, whichever comes first.

3 Every month check tyre pressures and inspect tyre treads; when high-speed touring the tyre pressures should be checked much more frequently, even to the extent of a daily check. If front wheel tread wear is uneven, check wheel alignment.

4 Every month check brake fluid level and battery acid level.

5 Owners are under a legal obligation to maintain all exterior lights in good working order, this also applies to headlamp beam setting, which should be checked at regular intervals by a Rover Distributor or Dealer.

Fuel recommendations The Rover $3\frac{1}{2}$ litre V8 engine is designed to run on 100 octane fuel, five star grade in the United Kingdom. See Owner's Instruction Manual for special advice when touring.

Lubricants The recommended lubricants have been found suitable for Rover cars and should be used whenever possible in the grades specified. When ordering oil, the correct grade, as well as the make, should be clearly stated.

The Rover Company attaches very great importance to the nature of the lubricants used in its products and therefore gives specific recommendations as detailed on the next page.

Should any of the recommended lubricants not be available in certain overseas territories, the Rover Distributor or Dealer for that territory will obtain specific guidance from The Rover Company, or owners may communicate with the Company where they so wish.

Engine Under adverse conditions, such as driving over dusty roads or where short stop-start runs are made, oil changes, attention to the engine flame traps and breather filter replacement must be more frequent.

Air Cleaner When the car is driven in dense city traffic or over dusty roads the elements should be changed more frequently.

Propeller shaft Under tropical or sandy and dusty conditions, the sliding joint must be lubricated frequently to prevent ingress of abrasive materials.

Rover parts

It is important that you should recognise the necessity of using only genuine Rover Parts or Rover Approved Parts when repair or maintenance work is being carried out on your car.

Rover parts are produced to the same high standard as those parts built into the car in its original production and it is in your best interests that you should insist that only genuine Rover Parts or Rover Approved Parts are fitted to your car.

Recommended lubricants and fluids

These recommendations apply to temperate climates where operational temperatures may vary between approximately —12°C (10°F) and 32°C (90°F).

Lubricants marked with an asterisk (*) are multigrade oils suitable for all temperature ranges.

Information on recommended lubricants for use under extreme winter or tropical conditions can be obtained from The Rover Co. Ltd, Technical Service Department, or your local Distributor or Dealer.

COMPONENTS	BP	CASTROL	DUCKHAM'S	ESSO	MOBIL	REGENT TEXACO/ CALTEX	SHELL
Engine	*BP Super Visco-Static 10W-40	*Castrol GTX	Duckham's Q20-50 Motor Oil	Uniflo or Esso Motor Oil 20W/50	Mobiloil Super	Havoline 20/20W	*Shell Super Oil
Automatic transmission and power steering	BP Autran B	Castrol TQF	Duckham's Q-Matic	Esso Glide	Mobil ATF 210	Texamatic Type F	Shell Donax T.7
Rear axle	BP Gear Oil SAE 90 EP	Castrol Hypoy	Duckham's Hypoid 90	Esso Gear Oil GX 90/140	Mobilube GX 90	Multigear Lubricant 90	Spirax 90 EP
Propeller shaft sliding spline, front hubs, rear spring and front torsion bar sleeves	BP Energrease L2	Castrol LM Grease	Duckham's LB10 Grease	Esso Multi-purpose Grease H	Mobilgrease MP or Mobilgrease Super	Marfak Multi-purpose	Retinax A or Darina AX
Brakes	Castrol Girling Brake and Clutch Fluid, Crimson, Specification J. 1703						
Anti-freeze solution for cooling system	Bluecol A A, coloured green, or any other anti-freeze solution conforming to British Standard No. 3150 or anti-freeze to MIL-E-5559 formulation. For summer and winter use						
Inhibitor solution for cooling system	Marston Lubricants SQ36—Coolant inhibitor concentrate. For summer use only if for any reason frost precautions are not required						

Routine maintenance

On the following pages, in the same general order as listed in the Maintenance Section of this book, will be found full instructions on how to carry out the maintenance and adjustments required on the Rover $3\frac{1}{2}$ litre models.

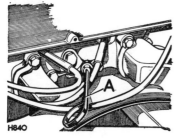

Engine oil level dipstick

A—Dipstick at left-hand side of engine

H840

Absolute cleanliness is essential when carrying out the maintenance work that follows.

Engine oil level—Every 1.000 km (750 miles)

Proceed as follows:

Stand the car on level ground and allow the oil to drain back into the sump. Withdraw the dipstick, wipe it clean, re-insert to its full depth and remove a second time to take the reading. Add oil as necessary through the screw-on filler cap on the right-hand front rocker cover. Never fill above the 'High' mark.

The oil filler cap with the dipstick attached at the right-hand rear of the engine is for the automatic transmission oil.

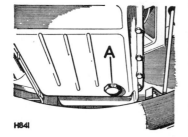

Engine sump drain plug

A—Drain plug at right-hand side of engine

H841

Engine oil changes and filter replacement—Every 8.000 km (5,000 miles) or every six months, whichever comes first

To change the engine oil:

Run the engine to warm up the oil, switch off the ignition. Remove the drain plug in the bottom of the sump. Allow oil to drain away completely and replace the plug.

To change filter:

1　Place oil tray under engine.

2　Unscrew the filter anticlockwise by the hexagon on end of casing.

3　Smear a little clean engine oil on the rubber washer of the new filter, then screw the filter on clockwise until the rubber sealing ring touches the oil pump cover face, then tighten a further half turn by hand only. Do not overtighten.

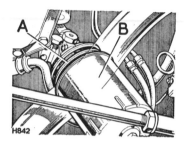

Engine oil filter

A—Washer for filter
B—Oil filter

Refill with oil of the correct grade through the screw-on filler cap on the right-hand front rocker cover; the capacity is 5,0 litres (9 Imperial pints), 10.5 US pints. This includes 0,5 litres (1 Imperial pint), 1.2 US pints for the filter.

Run engine and check for oil leaks at filter and drain plug.

Engine flame traps—Every 32.000 km (20,000 miles)

Clean as follows:

1　Remove the flame traps, one on top of each rocker cover by pulling off the hoses.

2　Wash by swilling in a dish of petrol.

3　Replace the flame traps, which are located in position by the hoses.

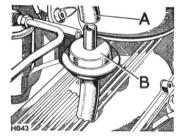

Engine flame trap

A—Hose
B—Flame trap

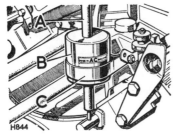

**Engine
breather filter**

A—Hose
B—Breather filter
C—Retaining clip

Engine breather filter—Every 32.000 km (20,000 miles)

Replace as follows:

1   Remove air cleaner, see following operation.

2   Disconnect hoses.

3   Slacken clip and withdraw filter.

4   Fit new filter, with the end marked 'IN' uppermost. Alternatively, if the filter is marked with arrows, they must point downwards.

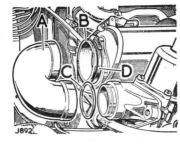

Air cleaner removal

A—Elbow for air
     cleaner
B—Hose, elbow to
     air cleaner
C—Seal, air cleaner
     elbow
D—Clip, elbow to
     air cleaner

Air cleaner—Every 16.000 km (10,000 miles)

Attention to the air cleaner is extremely important. Replace elements every 8.000 km (5,000 miles) under severe dusty conditions, as performance will be seriously affected if the car is run with an excessive amount of dust or industrial deposits in the element.

Proceed as follows:

1   Slacken off the two hose clips at each side of the air cleaner and release the two elbows.

2   Disconnect hose, engine breather filter to air cleaner, and the return petrol pipe clipped to the front of the air cleaner.

3 Unclip the cold-start cable from the air cleaner. Then remove the air cleaner body by easing it from over the domed retaining studs.

4 The elements can now be removed by releasing the three clips at each end of the air cleaner body. Withdraw end plates and elements. Unscrew wing nuts to release elements.

5 Discard old element and replace with new unit.

6 Ensure that the sealing washers on air cleaner and carburetter adaptors are in position and intact.

7 Reassemble by reversing the removal procedure.

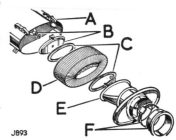

J893

Air cleaner element replacement

A—Clip for air cleaner body
B—Retainer and fixings for element
C—Sealing washer for element
D—Element
E—End plate for element
F—Hose clip and hose

Carburetter slow-running adjustment—Every 8.000 km (5,000 miles)

Carburetter adjustment should be carried out by a Rover Distributor or Dealer as special equipment is required.

Should the carburetters require adjustment for any reason, proceed as follows:

1 Set the gear selector at the 'P' (park) position.

2 Run the engine until normal operating temperature is obtained.

3 Remove air cleaner. See operation above.

4 Slacken screws securing throttle lever to carburetter lever on each carburetter.

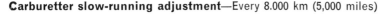

**Throttle lever
setting, right hand**

A—Screw fixing
throttle lever
and carburetter
lever, right hand

B—Lever with pin
for throttle link

C—Feeler gauge

D—Slow running
adjustment
screw

E—Fast idle adjust-
ment screw

F—Mixture adjust-
ment screw

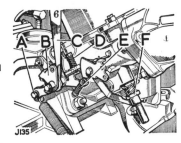

**Throttle lever
setting, left hand**

A—Countershaft
lever with nylon
roller

B—Throttle lever,
left hand

C—Fast idle adjust-
ment screw,
left hand

D—Slow running
adjustment
screw

E—Feeler gauge

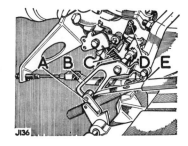

5 Using an approved carburetter throttle balancing device, turn the slow-running adjustment screws until an identical reading is obtained on both carburetters at an engine speed of 600-650 rpm.

6 Place a 0,15 mm (0.006 in.) feeler gauge between the right leg of the fork and the pin on the right-hand carburetter.

Apply light pressure to the linkage to hold the feeler, then tighten throttle lever securing screw.

7 Place a 0,15 mm (0.006 in.) feeler gauge between the lower side of the throttle roller and lever on the left-hand carburetter. Apply light pressure to the lever to hold the feeler, then tighten throttle lever securing screw.

8 The fast-idle screws should not require adjustment; however if adjustment becomes necessary, pull out the cold start control until the cold start warning light just comes on. Adjust fast idle adjustment screws until an identical reading is obtained on both carburetters with the balancing device, at an engine speed of 1,400 rpm. Push the cold start control in again.

9 Replace the air cleaner.

10 Check the mixture on each carburetter separately by lifting the carburetter piston approximately 1 mm (0.031 in.) by means of the lift pin situated on the front of the carburetter body. There is approximately 4,5 mm (0.187 in.) free movement of the lift pin before it contacts the piston.

11   If the engine speeds up immediately the mixture is too rich and the mixture adjustment nut must be screwed up, thus weakening the mixture; if the engine speed decreases immediately the mixture is too weak and the mixture adjustment nut should be unscrewed to enrich the mixture.

In either case turn one flat at a time and check after each adjustment.

If the engine speed momentarily increases very slightly the adjustment is correct.

12   Road test car for 5 km (3 miles) and stabilise carburetter temperature and repeat checks **10** and **11**. Re-check slow running adjustment. If incorrect, adjust by turning each slow running screw an equal amount.

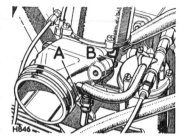

Carburetter mixture adjustment screw and lift pin

A—Mixture adjustment screw

B—Lift pin

Downshift cable adjustment—Every 8.000 km (5,000 miles) as part of carburetter adjustment procedure.

1   Chock vehicle front wheels and apply handbrake, also apply footbrake during the procedure.

2   Remove the line pressure take-off plug from the rear of the transmission case, using a suitable Allen key.

3   Connect the line pressure gauge to the pressure take-off point.

4   Connect the tachometer. If the tachometer in use is for 4 and 6 cylinder models, use the 4 cylinder position and note that the

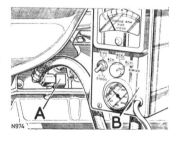

Pressure gauge connected to transmission

A—Line pressure take-off point

B—Line pressure gauge

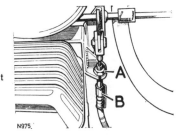

Transmission downshift cable

A—Adjuster locknut
B—Cable adjuster

N975

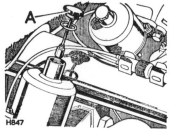

Carburetter hydraulic damper

A—Cap and hydraulic damper

H847

reading on the tachometer will be double the actual engine rpm, that is 500-550 will show as 1000-1100 rpm.

5 Start the engine and allow to warm up to the extent that it will idle evenly without the use of the choke control on fast idle position.

6 Select 'D' position with the selector lever and note reading on line pressure gauge.
The pressure should be:
At 1,000 rpm, 6,3 to 7,3 kg/cm^2 (90 to 105 lb/sq in.). If the pressure is less than 6,3 kg/cm^2 (90 lb/sq in.) at 1,000 rpm the pressure should be increased as follows:

7 Slacken the adjuster locknut on the transmission downshift cable.

8 Screw out the cable adjuster.

9 If the pressure is more than 7,3 kg/cm^2 (105 lb/sq in.) at 1,000 rpm, then the pressure should be decreased by screwing in the cable adjuster.

10 Tighten the adjuster locknut.

11 Switch off the engine. Disconnect the pressure gauge and replace the line pressure take-off plug, tighten the plug to a torque of 0,5 to 0,7 mkg (4 to 5 lb ft.).

Carburetter hydraulic dampers—Every 16.000 km (10,000 miles)

Unscrew the cap on top of each suction chamber, withdraw cap and hydraulic damper, replenish the damper reservoir as necessary with SAE 20 oil to within about 25 mm (1 in.) from the top of the tube. Then replace cap and hydraulic damper.

Automatic enrichment device, filter cleaning—Every 64.000 km (40,000 miles) when fitted

To clean nylon filter, float chamber lid and float chamber, proceed as follows:

1 Remove fuel inlet pipe and float chamber vent pipe.

2 Remove heat insulation cover.

3 Unscrew plug from float chamber lid and remove filter.

4 Remove three retaining screws and washers. Tap side of float chamber lid sharply with screwdriver handle if necessary to separate from gasket.

Carefully lift lid of float chamber and remove needle and float assembly. If the gasket is damaged or unserviceable cut along edge of body and remove float chamber portion. Do not remove screws holding top cover and valve body. Thoroughly clean float chamber lid and float chamber.

5 Examine float needle tip for wear or damage. Examine seating in lid. Replace any faulty parts.

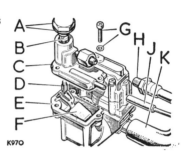

K970

Float chamber lid removal

A—Plug and washer for filter
B—Nylon filter
C—Float chamber lid
D—Needle
E—Gasket for float chamber. Cut at dotted line if replacement is required
F—Float
G—Screw and washer fixing float chamber lid
H—Fuel inlet pipe
J—Float chamber vent pipe
K—Air intake hose

Float replacement in lid

A—Float held against face of lid with feeler gauge or steel rule
B—Stirrup on float needle
C—Float
D—Float needle
E—Float chamber lid

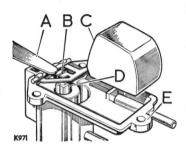

K97I

Float replacement in body

A—Plug and washer retaining nylon filter
B—Nylon filter
C—Screw and washer fixing float chamber lid
D—Float chamber lid
E—Float
F—Ensure hinge pin falls into recesses of body

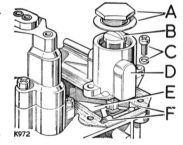

K972

6   Install float in main body and check for end-float of hinge pin in body and clearance around the float. Remove float.

7   If gasket has been cut and part removed, obtain a new float chamber and valve body gasket and cut and fit adjacent to the existing valve body gasket. Place cut gasket into position on main body.

8   Drop needle into seating of inverted float chamber lid. Then ensure the float needle is correctly located on float lever by wire stirrup.

Holding the float assembly to face of lid with the tip of steel rule or feeler gauge, position the lid over the float chamber close enough to allow the float assembly to be dropped so that the hinge pin falls into the recesses in the body without disengaging the needle from the seating bore.

Lower the lid on to the main body; align screw holes; fit three screws and spring washers and tighten.

9   Clean and then replace the filter in the float chamber lid. Using a new aluminium washer, refit plug and tighten.

Fuel filter, cartridge type—Replace every 16.000 km (10,000 miles)

The cartridge provides an additional filter between pump and carburetter.

Replace as follows:

1 Disconnect fuel pipes from each end of filter.

2 Slacken clip securing filter and withdraw unit.

3 Fit new filter with flange uppermost, tighten securing clip and refit fuel pipes.

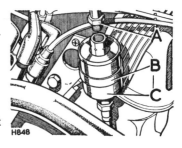

Fuel filter, cartridge type

A—Fuel pipe
B—Clip
C—Fuel filter

Sparking plugs—Check every 8.000 km (5,000 miles); replace every 16.000 km (10,000 miles)

Use the special sparking plug spanner and tommy bar supplied in the tool kit when removing or refitting sparking plugs.

IMPORTANT—Take great care when fitting sparking plugs not to cross-thread the plug otherwise costly damage to the cylinder head will result.

Check or replace the sparking plugs as applicable; if the plugs are in good condition clean and re-set the electrode gaps to 0,60 mm (0.025 in.), at the same time file the end of the central electrode until bright metal can be seen.

It is important that only Champion L87Y sparking plugs are used for replacements.

Sparking plug

A—Sparking plug

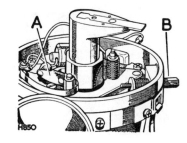

**Distributor
contact points**

A—Contact points
B—Adjuster for
   contact points

Distributor contact points—Every 16.000 km (10,000 miles)

To obtain satisfactory engine performance it is most important that the contact points are adjusted to the dwell angle which is 26° – 28° using suitable workshop equipment. This work should be carried out by your local Rover Distributor or Dealer.

However, if it becomes necessary to change the contact points, and specialised checking equipment is not available, they may be adjusted as follows:

1 Remove the distributor cap; then turn the engine, using a 0.937 in. ($\frac{15}{16}$ in.) AF socket spanner on the front pulley retaining bolt, until the contacts are fully open.

2 The clearance should be 0,35 to 0,40 mm (0.014 to 0.016 in.) with the feeler gauge a sliding fit between the contacts.

3 Adjust by turning the adjusting nut clockwise to increase gap and anticlockwise to reduce gap.

4 Replace the distributor cap.

IMPORTANT At the first available opportunity after the contact points have been adjusted as detailed above they must be finally set to the dwell angle using specialised equipment. At the same time check the ignition timing which should be dynamically set to 6° BTDC at 500–600 rpm.

Distributor maintenance—Every 16.000 km (10,000 miles)

Lubricate as follows:

1 Remove the distributor cap and rotor arm.

2 Lightly smear the cam with clean engine oil.

3 Add a few drops of thin machine oil to lubricate the cam bearing and distributor shaft. See illustration.

4 Add a few drops of thin machine oil through the hole in the contact breaker base plate, to lubricate the automatic timing control. See illustration.

5 Remove the nut on the terminal block and lift off the spring and moving contact, also remove adjustable contact secured with a screw and nut. Ensure that the contacts are free from grease or oil; if they are burned or blackened, clean with a fine carborundum stone and wipe with a petrol-moistened cloth. Add a smear of grease to contact pivot before replacing the contacts. Then adjust as detailed in previous operation.

6 Wipe the inside and outside of the cap with a soft dry cloth; ensure that the small carbon brush works freely in its holder.

7 Replace rotor arm and distributor cap.

8 Adjust contact points. Dwell angle 26°–28°.

9 Check ignition setting: 6° BTDC at 500–600 rpm.

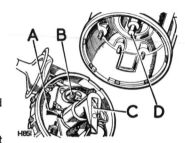

Distributor

A—Lubricate at this point
B—Contact breaker lever pivot
C—Rotor arm
D—Carbon brush

Fluid level dipstick-plug in engine compartment

A—Dipstick
B—Tube for dipstick

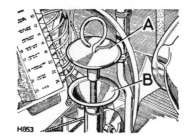

H853

Fluid level dipstick

A—Transmission cold, top-up to upper mark on 'COLD' side of dipstick

B—Transmission hot, top-up to upper mark on 'HOT' side of dipstick

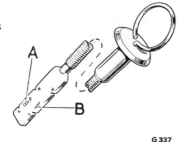

G 337

Automatic transmission fluid level—Every 8.000 km (5,000 miles)

The torque converter and automatic gearbox are lubricated as one unit. As the fluid for operating the torque converter is fed from the transmission casing it is essential when checking the level or topping-up the automatic gearbox that the engine is run at idling speed for about two minutes to transfer fluid from transmission casing to torque converter, otherwise a false level reading will be obtained. Do not add anti-friction additives to the automatic transmission fluid. Check as follows:

1 Absolute cleanliness is essential. Use only nylon rag for cleaning.

2 Stand car on level ground. Engine idling and selector at the 'P' position.

3 Lift bonnet to expose dipstick which is at the rear of the air cleaner.

4 Clean area around dipstick hole. Remove dipstick, wipe dry and check fluid level. Take the dipstick reading immediately after the dipstick has been fully inserted to avoid misreadings by splashing. The difference between full and low marks on dipstick represents approximateley 0,5 litre (one pint). See paragraph 6.

5 With the engine idling and the selector at 'P', add the recommended grade of fluid to bring the level up to the 'full' mark. Do not overfill.

6 When the transmission is hot, top-up to the upper mark on the side of the dipstick marked 'HOT'. With transmission cold, top-up to the upper mark on the side of the dipstick marked 'COLD'. It is most important to ascertain if the transmission is hot or cold when

topping up and to use the appropriate mark, otherwise over-filling or under-filling will result.

7   If significant topping-up is required check for leakage at oil seals and sump joint, rectify immediately.

Rear axle differential oil level—Every 8.000 km (5,000 miles)

Check oil level and top-up if necessary to the bottom of the filler plug hole. Access to this plug is gained from underneath the car.

If significant topping-up is required check for oil leaks at plugs, joint faces and oil seals adjacent to axle shaft flanges and propeller shaft driving flange.

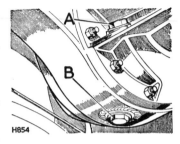

Rear axle differential oil level-filler plug and drain plug

A—Oil level-filler plug

B—Drain plug

Rear axle differential oil changes—Every 32.000 km (20,000 miles)

To change the differential oil, proceed as follows:

Immediately after a run, when the oil is warm, drain off the oil by removing the drain plug in the bottom of the casing. Replace the drain plug, remove filler-level plug and refill with oil of the correct grade; the capacity is approximately 1,75 litres (3 Imperial pints), 3.5 US pints.

Power steering box lubrication—Every 1.000 km (750 miles) and at every maintenance inspection

The power steering units are lubricated by the operating fluid. The only lubrication maintenance required is to check the reservoir fluid level and if necessary top-up to the 'F' mark on dipstick, using one of the recommended grades of fluid.

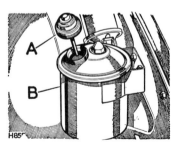

Oil filler cap and dipstick

A—Oil filler cap and dipstick

B—Reservoir

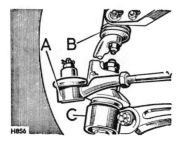

Ball joints

A—Steering ball
    joint
B—Steering ball
    swivel, upper
C—Steering ball
    swivel, lower

If significant topping-up is required check for oil leaks at hose connections, rocker shaft and camshaft oil seals and joint faces on steering unit and power steering pump.

Steering swivel and ball joints—Every 16.000 km (10,000 miles)

The steering joints have been designed to retain the initial filling of grease for the normal life of the ball joints; however, this applies only if the rubber boot remains in the correct position. Check to ensure that the rubber boots have not become dislodged or damaged, and check for wear in the joint.

This can be done by moving the ball joint vigorously up and down. Should there be any appreciable free movement the complete joint must be replaced.

Fan belt adjustment

A—Adjusting bolt
B—Pivot bolts
C—Check at this
    point 11 to 14 mm
    (0.437 to 0.562 in.)
    free movement

Fan and power steering pump belt adjustment—Every 16.000 km (10,000 miles)

Check by thumb pressure between the pump and crankshaft pulleys and between alternator and crankshaft pulleys at point marked 'C'. Movement should be:

Fan belt	11 to 14 mm (0.437 to 0.562 in.)
Power steering pump belt	6 to 9 mm (0.25 to 0.312 in.)

If necessary adjust as follows:

Fan belt

1 Slacken the bolts securing the alternator to the front cover and the adjustment link.

2 Pivot the alternator inwards or outwards as necessary and adjust until the correct tension is obtained.

3 Tighten alternator adjusting bolts.

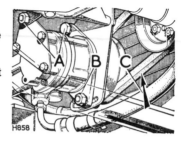

Power steering pump belt adjustment

A—Pivot bolts
B—Adjusting bolt
C—Check at this point 6 to 9 mm (0.25 to 0.312 in.) free movement

Power steering pump belt—This operation must be carried out from underneath the vehicle

1 Slacken the pivot bolts securing the power steering pump to the mounting bracket, slacken the adjusting bolt.

2 Pivot the pump inwards or outwards as necessary and adjust until the correct belt tension is obtained.

3 Tighten adjusting and pivot bolts.

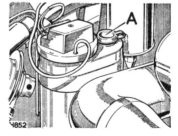

Windscreen washer reservoir

A—Filler cap

Water level, windscreen washer—Every 8.000 km (5,000 miles)

Top-up reservoir to within 12 mm (0.5 in.) below bottom of filler neck. In cold weather, to prevent freezing of the water, the reservoir should have Isopropyl Alcohol added to the water.

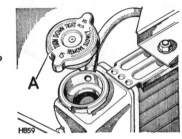

Radiator filler cap

A—Filler cap

Radiator water level—Every 1.000 km (750 miles) and at every maintenance inspection

To prevent corrosion of the aluminium alloy engine parts it is imperative that the cooling system is filled with a solution of water and anti-freeze, winter or summer, or water and inhibitor during the summer only. Never fill or top-up with plain water otherwise damage to the engine will result.

The radiator filler cap is under the bonnet panel.

With a cold engine the correct water level is 25 mm (1 inch) below the bottom of the filler neck.

Warning: The cooling system is pressurised and great care must be taken when removing the radiator filler cap, when the engine is hot, otherwise personal scalding could result.

When removing the filler cap, first turn it anticlockwise to the stop and allow all pressure to escape, before pressing it down and turning further in the same direction to lift it off.

When replacing the filler cap it is important that it is tightened down fully, not just to the first stop. Failure to tighten the filler cap properly may result in water loss, with possible damage to the engine through overheating.

If the cooling system is being refilled after draining or a large quantity of water needs to be added proceed as follows:

1   Place the left-hand heater lever at the 'hot' position.
2   Pull up knob on the rear heater valve.
3   Fill radiator with a solution of either water and anti-freeze or water and inhibitor. See next item for details of anti-freeze and inhibitor solutions and quantity to be used.
4   Push knob down on rear heater valve.

5 Run engine at a fast idle until top radiator hose is warm, that is thermostat open.

6 With engine still running at a fast idle fill radiator to the bottom of the neck of the filler tube.

7 Place left-hand heater lever at the 'off' position. Pull up knob on the rear heater valve. Run engine at fast idle for one minute to purge air from rear car heater. Place left-hand heater at the 'hot' position.

8 Top-up system to bottom of radiator filler neck with engine idling. It is essential to again check the water level and top-up if necessary when the engine has attained normal running temperature.

9 The water level will fall to 25 mm (1 in.) below the bottom of the filler neck when engine is cold.

IMPORTANT During the warm-up period of the filling procedure the radiator filler cap should be removed only when the engine is **idling.**

Use soft water wherever possible; if the local water supply is hard, rainwater should be used.

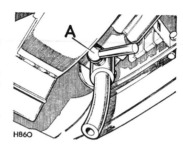

Radiator drain plug

A—Drain plug, under valance at right-hand side

Frost precautions and engine protection

During the winter and summer months a special anti-freeze mixture is used in Rover 3½ litre cars to prevent corrosion of the aluminium alloy engine parts. **It is most important therefore if the cooling system is drained at any time, to refill with a solution of water and anti-freeze during winter and summer, or water and inhibitor during the summer only.**

Recommended solutions are:

Anti-freeze—Bluecol AA, coloured green, or any other anti-freeze solution conforming to British Standard 3150.

Inhibitor—Marston Lubricants SQ36. Coolant inhibitor concentrate.

Use one part of anti-freeze to two parts of water.

Use 3 fluid ounces of inhibitor per 4,5 litres (one gallon) of water.

Cylinder block drain tap

A—Drain tap, two fitted, one each side of engine

To ensure that the solution is fully effective at all times the cooling system should be drained and refilled every twelve months.

Proceed as follows:

1 Ensure that the cooling system is leak-proof; anti-freeze solutions are far more 'searching' at joints than water.

2 Drain and flush the system.

3 Pour in approximately 4,5 litres (one gallon) of water, add solution. 3 litres (5.3 pints) of anti-freeze, summer or winter, or 170 millilitres (6 fluid ounces) of inhibitor if frost protection is not required. Then top-up as detailed under 'Radiator water level'.

During the winter and summer months Rover 3½ litre cars leaving the Rover factory have the cooling system filled with 33% of anti-freeze mixture. This gives protection against frost down to minus 32°C (25°F).

Cars so filled can be identified by the green label affixed to the right-hand side of the windscreen and a green label tied to the engine.

Front hub lubrication

A—Check for leakage at these points

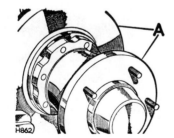

Front hub lubrication—Every 16.000 km (10,000 miles)

Check front hubs for leakage. This may be seen at disc shield or inside wheel rim.

If there are signs of leakage at the above points, the necessary rectification should be carried out by a Rover Distributor or Dealer.

Wheel alignment—Every 32.000 km (20,000 miles)

Special equipment is required to check wheel alignment and this work should be carried out by your local Rover Distributor or Dealer.

For those owners who have suitable equipment, the alignment should be 1,5 mm (0.062 in.) toe-in to 1,5 mm (0.062 in.) toe-out.

To adjust, slacken the locknuts of the steering track rod and turn to obtain the correct alignment. Tighten locknuts and re-check. Ensure that the track rod ball joints are correctly aligned; that is, the top of the ball joint should be horizontal in the fore and aft direction.

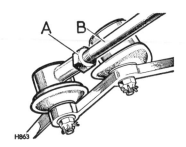

Adjustment for wheel alignment

A—Locknut
B—Steering track rod

Brake fluid reservoir—Every month and at every maintenance inspection

The reservoir cap incorporates a float and level switch which operates the amber brake warning light, should the level in the reservoir fall below the safe limit.

Check fluid level in brake reservoir, top-up if necessary to rib on reservoir. Use Castrol Girling Crimson Brake and Clutch Fluid (Specification J. 1703).

If significant topping-up is required check master cylinder, brake disc and wheel cylinders and brake pipes for leakage; any leakage must be rectified immediately.

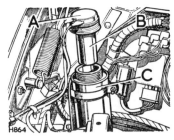

Brake fluid reservoir

A—Cap
B—Float unit
C—Reservoir

When removing reservoir cap do not disconnect the wires; care should be taken when withdrawing the float unit to ensure that the brake fluid does not drip on to the car.

Check operation of reservoir level safety switch as follows:

Ignition 'on', hand brake 'off': unscrew and lift filler cap 25 mm (1 in.), warning light should be illuminated.

If the warning light is not illuminated, the operation of the float unit and the wiring connections must be investigated

Front brake pads—Every 8.000 km (5,000 miles)

Hydraulic disc brakes are fitted at the front, and the correct brake adjustment is automatically maintained; no provision is therefore made for adjustment.

Check the thickness of the foot brake pads and renew if the minimum thickness is less than 3 mm (0.125 in.), also check for oil contamination on brake pads and discs.

This operation should be carried out from underneath the car.

If replacement or rectification is necessary this should be carried out by a Rover Distributor or Dealer.

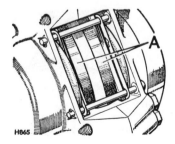

Checking foot brake pads

A—Foot brake pads, minimum thickness 3 mm (0.125 in.)

H865

Rear brake shoes—Every 8.000 km (5,000 miles)

Check and if necessary adjust the rear brake shoes as follows by means of the single adjuster at the forward side of the brake anchor plate:

1   With the rear wheels jacked up, ensure that they rotate freely; slacken the adjuster if necessary, by turning anticlockwise.

2   Apply the foot brake to ensure that the shoes are bedded in and turn the adjuster clockwise until the linings brush the brake drum, then slacken adjuster off two clicks.

   This also adjusts the handbrake.

Rear wheel brake adjustment

A—Adjuster

Bleeding the brake system

If the brakes feel spongy, this may be caused by air in the hydraulic system. This air must be removed by bleeding the hydraulic system at each wheel cylinder. Bleeding must always be carried out at all wheels.

1   Attach a length of rubber tubing to the bleed nipple on the wheel cylinder farthest from the brake pedal and place the lower end of the tube in a glass jar containing brake fluid.

2   Slacken the bleed screw and pump the brake pedal slowly, pausing at end of each return stroke, until the fluid issuing from the tube shows no signs of air bubbles when the tube is held below the surface of the fluid in the jar.

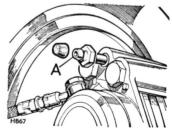

Brake bleed nipple

A—Bleed nipple

3 Hold the tube under the fluid surface and, with the foot brake fully depressed, tighten the bleed screw.

4 Repeat for the other three wheels in turn, finishing at the one nearest the brake pedal.

The fluid in the reservoir should be replenished throughout the operation to prevent another air lock being formed, using only new fluid. Castrol Girling Crimson Brake and Clutch Fluid (Specification J. 1703).

It will be obvious that the above operation requires two people.

Fluid changing, brake system—Every eighteen months

5 All fluid in the brake system should be changed every eighteen months. It should also be changed before touring in mountainous areas if not done in the previous nine months. Use only Castrol Girling Crimson Brake and Clutch Fluid (Specification J. 1703).

Rubber seals in brake system—Every 64.000 km (40,000 miles) or every three years whichever comes first

Renew all rubber seals in master cylinder, wheel cylinders and caliper pistons. Refill with correct fluid, that is, Castrol Girling Crimson Brake and Clutch Fluid (Specification J. 1703).

The above work must be carried out by your local Rover Distributor or Dealer.

Changing wheel positions—Every 8.000 km (5,000 miles)

The road wheels should be changed round as illustrated, to equalise tyre wear.

Finally, ensure road wheel nuts are tight.

Tyre pressures—Every month and at every maintenance attention

Maximum tyre life and performance will be obtained only if the tyres are maintained at the correct pressures.

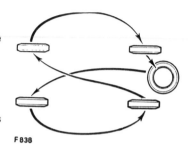

Changing wheel positions

F 838

	Normal loads		Fully laden	
	Front	Rear	Front	Rear
Speeds up to 168 kph (105 mph)				
kg/cm^2	1,8	1,8	1,8	2,2
lb/sq in.	26	26	26	32
Bars	1.79	1.79	1.79	2.21
Speeds over 168 kph (105 mph)				
kg/cm^2	2,1	2,1	2,1	2,4
lb/sq in.	30	30	30	34
Bars	2.07	2.07	2.07	2.34

Whenever possible check with the tyres cold, as the pressure is about 0,2 kg/cm^2 (3 lb/sq in.) 0.21 Bars higher at running temperature.

Always replace valve caps, they form a positive seal on the valves.

When high-speed touring, the tyre pressures should be checked much more frequently, even to the extent of a daily check.

If front wheel tread wear is uneven, check wheel alignment.

Any unusual pressure loss in excess of 0,05 kg/cm² (1 lb/sq in.) 0.07 Bars per week should be investigated and corrected.

Always check the spare wheel, so that it is ready for use at any time.

At the same time, remove embedded flints, etc. from the tyre treads with the aid of a penknife or similar tool. Clean off any oil or grease on the tyres, using petrol sparingly.

Check that there are no lumps or bulges in the tyres, or exposure of the ply or cord structure.

Minimum tread depth 1 mm in the United Kingdom but may be subject to local safety regulations in other countries.

Wheel and tyre units are accurately balanced on initial assembly with the aid of clip-on weights secured to the wheel rims.

Wheel balance should always be checked whenever new tyres are fitted to ensure that the dynamic balance of the wheel and tyre is correct.

When tyres are changed, road wheels should be carefully checked for possible damage.

When replacements are required the tyres should be as currently specified by the Company. They should be of the same type and make as those previously fitted.

In the case of tubeless tyres a new Schrader snap-in valve must be fitted whenever a tubeless tyre is replaced.

Propeller shaft lubrication—Every 8.000 km (5,000 miles)

Apply one of the recommended greases at the lubrication nipple on the sliding portion of rear propeller shaft.

Fully-sealed journals are fitted and these require no lubrication.

Propeller shaft lubrication

A—Lubrication nipple

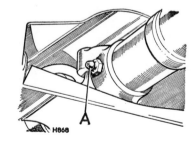

H868

Battery acid level—Every month and at every maintenance attention

The battery is located in the luggage boot at the right-hand side under a metal cover. Check acid level as follows:

1 Remove the battery cover by releasing the locating clips.

2 Wipe all dirt and moisture from the battery top.

3 Remove the filler cover. If necessary add sufficient distilled water to raise the level to the top of separators. Replace the filler cover.

Avoid the use of a naked light when examining the cells.

4 Replace battery cover and retain by means of the clips.

In hot climates it will be necessary to top-up the battery at more frequent intervals.

In very cold weather it is essential that the car is used immediately after topping-up, to ensure that the distilled water is thoroughly mixed with the electrolyte. Neglect of this precaution may result in the distilled water freezing and causing damage to the battery.

The specific gravity of the electrolyte should also be checked at every maintenance attention.

Readings should be:

Temperate climates below 26.5°C (80°F) as commissioned for service, fully charged 1.270 to 1.290 specific gravity.

As expected during normal service three-quarter charged 1.230 to 1.250 specific gravity.

If the specific gravity should read between 1.190 to 1.210, half-charged, the battery must be bench charged and the electrical equipment on the car should be checked.

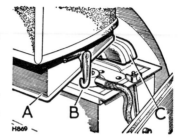

Battery acid level

A—Battery cover
B—Securing clip
C—Filler cover

Tropical climate, above 26.5°C (80°F) as commissioned for service, fully charged 1.210 to 1.230 specific gravity.

As expected during normal service three-quarter charged 1.170 to 1.190 specific gravity.

If the specific gravity should read between 1.130 to 1.150, half-charged, the battery must be bench charged and the electrical equipment on the car should be checked.

Battery terminals—Every 16.000 km (10,000 miles)

Remove battery terminals, clean, grease and refit. Replace terminal screw, do not overtighten. Do not use the screw for pulling down the terminal.

Headlamp and fog lamp beam setting—Every 16.000 km (10,000 miles)

This operation is best done with special equipment and should be carried out by your local Rover Distributor or Dealer.

Oil-can lubrication—Every 16.000 km (10,000 miles)

Apply a few spots of oil to throttle linkage, hand brake linkage, door locks, etc.

PART TWO
GENERAL INFORMATION

This section of the book gives details of headlamp light unit and bulb changing, circuit diagram, seat adjustment and jacking points, etc.

Headlamps

To replace light unit or bulb:

1 Insert a screwdriver under the rim at the bottom of the lamp and gently lever off the rim. Take care not to damage the paintwork.

2 Remove the dust excluder retained by three recessed-head screws.

3 Sealed-beam type: Withdraw the headlamp unit and disconnect the plug at the rear. Replace the unit and reassemble.

4 Replacement bulb type: Press in the light unit against the tension of the springs on the three adjustment screws, turn it anticlockwise and withdraw. Release spring clips and move bulb holder; the bulb can then be replaced and the unit reassembled.

5 All types: Ensure that the headlamp rim is pushed right on to the retaining clips.

Fog lamps

To replace light unit:

1 Slacken retaining screw.

2 Withdraw rim complete with light unit

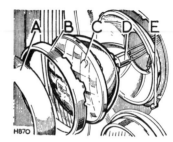

Headlamp light unit replacement

A—Retaining rim
B—Dust excluder
C—Light unit
D—Plug at rear of light unit
E—Insert screwdriver at this point

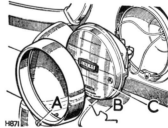

Fog lamps

A—Retaining screw for rim
B—Clip retaining light unit
C—Light unit

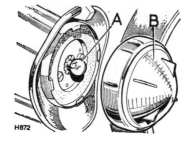

Side lamp bulb replacement

A—Bulb
B—White lens

3　Disconnect leads from light unit

4　Release spring clips and separate light unit from rim.

5　Fit new light unit, then reverse removal procedure.

Wing lamps

To replace side lamp or flasher lamp bulb.

Side lamps:

1　Turn the rim in an anticlockwise direction, and withdraw complete with lens.

2　Renew the bulb, ensure that the washers are in position and refit the lens and rim.

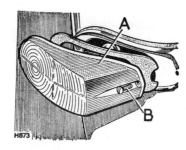

Flasher lamp bulb replacement

A—Amber lens
B—Retaining screw

Flasher lamps:

1　Remove the retaining screws and withdraw the lens.

2　Renew bulb and replace lens; ensure washer is in position, then secure with the retaining screws.

Rear lamps

To replace flasher, stop/tail or number plate illumination bulbs.

Stop/tail and flasher lamp:

1   Remove retaining screw and lift off the rim.

2   Remove appropriate lens; upper amber for the direction indicator lights, lower red for the stop/tail light. Renew bulb.

3   To replace, locate the lens in the rubber bead.

4   Slip the rim over the retaining clip at the top and replace the securing screw. Ensure that the rubber bead fits snugly round the rim.

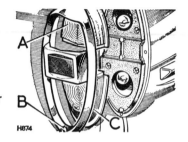

Rear lamp bulb replacement

A—Amber lens
B—Retaining screw for rim
C—Red lens

Number plate illumination and reversing lamp:

1   Remove two retaining screws and lift off top cover.

2   Remove lens.

3   If necessary, slightly withdraw bulb holder and replace bulb as required.

4   Push bulb holder into position, replace lens and retain by means of the top cover and securing screws.

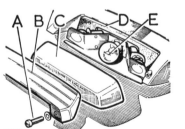

Number plate illumination and reversing lamp

A—Retaining screw for rim
B—Cover
C—Glass
D—Number plate illumination bulbs
E—Reverse light bulb

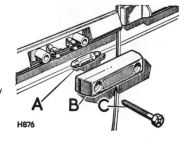

Repeater flasher

A—Festoon bulb
B—Amber lens
C—Retaining screw

H876

Repeater flasher

To replace bulb:

1   Remove two screws securing lens.

2   Renew bulb and replace lens; ensure washer is in position, then secure with the retaining screws.

**Interior light
bulb replacement**

A—Festoon bulb
B—Retaining screws
C—Cover

H877

Interior lights

To replace interior light bulbs. One lamp above each door:

1   Remove two screws retaining cover.

2   Replace bulb and refit cover.

Instrument panel and warning lights

To replace any of the light bulbs:

1   Remove two screws from underside of panel.

2   Swing panel upwards and forwards.

3   Replace bulb as required and refit panel.

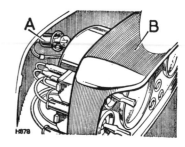

Panel and warning light bulb replacement

A—Bulb holder
B—Panel

Clock

To replace clock illumination bulb:

1   Slacken screw beneath clock at underside of facia rail and withdraw clock.

2   Remove bulb holder and replace bulb.

3   Reverse removal procedure.

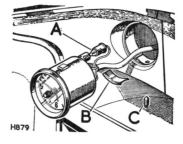

Clock illumination bulb replacement

A—Bulb holder
B—Fixing screw
C—Clock

Clock adjustment

A—Clock losing,
   turn to + mark
B—Clock gaining,
   turn to — mark

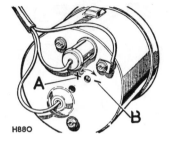

H880

To regulate clock:

1 Remove clock, as above.

2 Adjust as required by means of screw at rear of clock.

   Clock gaining: turn to — mark

   Clock losing: turn to + mark

This regulation should be attempted only if the clock gains or loses more than two or three minutes per week.

Cigar lighter

A—Cigar lighter
B—Bulb holder
C—Bulb
D—Retainer for
   bulb holder
E—Consol unit

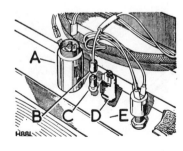

H881

Cigar lighter illumination

To replace bulb:

   Front:

1 Remove the two bolts securing the consol unit, pull unit forward and down.

2 Disconnect leads from cigar lighter.

3 Compress sides of bulb retainer and withdraw unit complete with bulb.

4 Renew bulb, then reverse removal procedure.

Rear: Coupé only.

1 Lift ashtray lid, withdraw ashtray.

2 Remove two screws retaining ashtray holder and lift out.

3 Compress sides of bulb retainer and withdraw unit complete with bulb.

4 Renew bulb then reverse removal procedure.

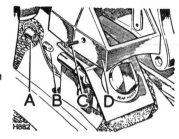

Rear heater switch

A—Bulb holder
B—Bulb
C—Screw fixing cover
D—Switch cover

Rear heater switch illumination

To replace bulb:

1 Remove three screws and lift off switch cover.

2 Withdraw bulb holder.

3 Renew bulb, refit holder and replace cover.

Automatic transmission indicator plate illumination bulb

To replace bulb:

1 Unclip indicator plate from gear selector surround.

2 Renew bulb and clip indicator plate back on to the surround.

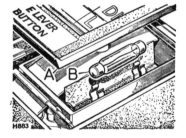

Automatic transmission indicator plate illumination bulb replacement

A—Indicator plate
B—Festoon bulb

Bonnet light bulb replacement

A—Bulb
B—Glass cover
C—Retaining screws

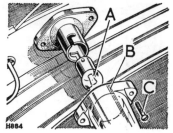

Bonnet light—Coupé models

To replace either of the bonnet light bulbs:

1   Lift the bonnet, then remove two screws retaining glass cover.

2   Replace bulb and refit cover.

Boot light

A—Bulb holder
B—Bulb

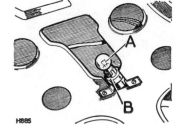

Boot light, underside of boot lid

To replace bulb:

1   Lift boot lid.

2   Remove and replace bulb as required.

Additional instruments—Coupé models

To replace instrument bulb:

1 Slacken screw beneath instrument and withdraw unit.

2 Withdraw the rubber sleeve and bulb holder from the rear of the instrument body.

3 Replace bulb and reverse removal procedure.

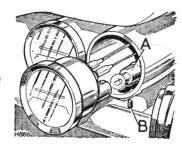

Instrument bulb replacement Coupé models

A—Bulb holder
B—Securing screw

Fuses

The fuses are located on the bulkhead under the bonnet. To replace a fuse:

1 The cover, which indicates the function of each fuse, should be pulled off.

2 Replace fuse as required:

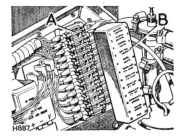

Fuse block

A—Fuses
B—Cover

Fuse Number	Fuse Protects	Fuse, Amps
1–2	Battery control, that is, clock, cigar lighters, interior lights, headrest light	35
3–4	Ignition control, that is, stop, reverse and flasher lights, screen washer, water temperature and fuel gauges, tachometer, automatic transmission inhibitor switch, oil pressure transmitter ..	25
5–6	Parking lights	5
7–8	Side and tail lights	5
9–10	Panel lights	5
11–12	Headlamp RH main beam	15
13–14	Headlamp LH main beam	15
15–16	Headlamp RH dip beam	10
17–18	Headlamp LH dip beam	10
19–20	Screenwiper motor	15
21–22	Heater motor	15
23–24	Fog lamp	25
—	In-line fuse for heated backlight	25

3   Ensure correct replacement is used as detailed above. Replace cover.

A spare 15 amp, 25 amp and 35 amp fuse will be found in the fuse block cover.

Continental lighting

Changes of lighting for Continental touring may be required. Advice on the best procedure can be obtained from The Rover Company Limited, Technical Service Department.

Jacking the car

Four tubular jacking brackets are fitted under the body lower rail, behind the front wheels and just in front of the rear wheels.

To raise one corner of the car:

1 Remove the rubber dust excluder from the appropriate jacking point.

2 Fit the pivoted extension on the jack into the tube up to the stop on the extension. This extension can be lowered or raised by turning the handle either one way or the other.

3 Turn the handle until the road wheel is clear of the ground.

To lower the car, reverse these operations.

If it is desired to raise the car with means other than those supplied, suitable jacking points are:

Front: Under the centre of the front cross-member.

Rear: Under the axle casing.

Jacking the car

A—Jack
B—Rubber plug

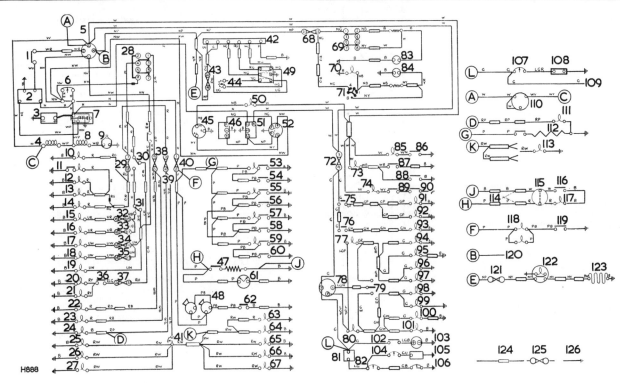

Circuit diagram, models with manual cotd start control, RH and LH Steering

H888

Key to circuit diagram, models with manual cold start control, RH and LH Steering

1 Inhibitor switch
2 Relay for starter motor
3 Battery
4 Ballast resistance
5 Switch, ignition and starter
6 Ammeter
7 Starter motor
8 Ignition coil
9 Distributor
10 Side lamp, left hand RHD, right hand LHD
11 Switch and lamp, boot
12 } Rear number plate
13 } illumination
14 Tail lamp, left hand RHD, right hand LHD
15 Headlamp, RH, dip beam
16 Headlamp, LH, dip beam
17 Headlamp, RH, main beam
18 Headlamp, LH, main beam
19 Warning light, main beam
20 Fog lamp, RH
21 Fog lamp, LH
22 Tail lamp, (park) right hand RHD, left hand LHD
23 Side lamp, (park) right hand RHD, left hand LHD
24 Cigar lighter, front, illumination
25 } Panel
26 } illumination, LH
27 Speedometer illumination
28 Switch, side, tail and park lamps
29 Fuse, 7–8 (5 amp), side and tail lights
30 Switch, headlamp, on steering column
31 Switch, headlamp dip
32 Fuse, 15–16 (10 amp), headlamp RH dip
33 Fuse, 17–18 (10 amp), headlamp LH dip
34 Fuse, 11–12 (15 amp), headlamp RH main
35 Fuse, 13–14 (15 amp), headlamp LH main
36 Switch, fog lamp
37 Fuse, 23–24, fog lamps
38 Fuse, 5–6 (5 amp), parking lights
39 Fuse, 9–10 (5 amp), panel lights
40 Fuse, 1–2 (35 amp), battery control
41 Switch, panel illumination
42 Screen wiper motor
43 Fuse, 19–20 (15 amp)

44 Switch, rheostat, screen wiper
45 Relay 3AW, warning lights
46 Control 4TR, alternator
47 Cigar lighter and switch
48 Horns
49 Switch, screen wiper
50 Warning light, ignition
51 Relay 6RA, alternator
52 Alternator, 11 AC
53 Interior lamp and switch, front, LH
54 Switch, front door, LH
55 Interior lamp and switch, rear, LH
56 Switch, rear door, LH
57 Interior lamp and switch, rear, RH
58 Switch, rear door, RH
59 Interior lamp and switch, front, RH
60 Switch, front door, RH
61 Clock
62 Switch, horns
63 Clock illumination
64 Gear selector illumination
65 } Panel
66 } illumination, RH
67 Grouped instrument illumination
68 Fuse, 21–22 (25 amp), heater motor
69 Switch, heater, front
70 Heater illumination, rear
71 Switch, heater, rear
72 Fuse, 3–4 (25 amp), ignition control
73 Warning light, brake fluid level and hand brake
74 Warning light, cold start
75 Switch, stop light
76 Switch, reverse light
77 Warning light, RH, direction indicators
78 Direction indicator unit
79 Switch, headlamp flasher
79 Switch, direction indicators
80 Warning light, LH, direction indicators
81 Regulator, 10 volt
82 Gauge, fuel
83 Heater motor, two-speed, front
84 Heater motor, two-speed, rear
85 Warning light, oil pressure
86 Switch, oil pressure

87 Switch, hand brake
88 Switch, brake fluid level
89 Switch, cold start
90 Thermostat, cold start
91 Stop light, RH
92 Stop light, LH
93 Reverse light
94 Direction indicator, front LH
95 Repeater director indicator, LH front
96 Repeater direction indicator, LH rear
97 Direction indicator, rear, LH
98 Direction indicator, rear, RH
99 Repeater direction indicator, RH rear
100 Repeater direction indicator, RH front
101 Direction indicator, front, RH
102 Switch, windscreen washer
103 Windscreen washer
104 Gauge, water temperature
105 Transmitter, water temperature
106 Tank unit, fuel
107 Gauge, oil pressure
108 Transmitter, oil pressure
109 To screen washer switch
110 Tachometer
111 Rear cigar lighter illumination
112 Cigar lighter
113 Nacelle illumination, four lamps
} Coupé
114 Pick-up point when two lamps are fitted
115 Plug and socket, headrest lamp
116 Switch, headrest lamp
117 Headrest lamp
118 Bonnet lamp*
119 Switch, bonnet lamp*
120 Radio pick-up
121 Fuse (25 amp) in line, heated backlight
122 Switch, illuminated, heated backlight
123 Heated backlight
124 Snap and Lucar connections
125 Fuses
126 Earth connections
} Optional equipment

* Standard on coupé

Encircled letters on circuit diagram show pick-up points for additional and optional equipment.

CABLE COLOUR CODE: B—Black   P—Purple   W—White   R—Red   N—Brown   Y—Yellow   U—Blue   G—Green   L—Light

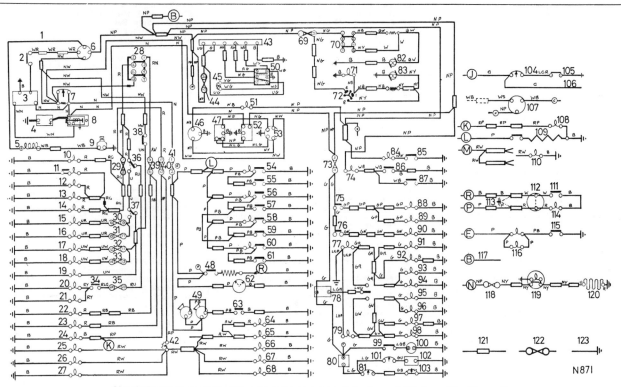

Circuit diagram, models with automatic enrichment device and thief-proof ignition coil

N871

Key to circuit diagram, models fitted with automatic enrichment device and thief-proof ignition coil, RH and LH Steering

1 Thief-proof ignition coil lead	41 Fuse, 1–2 (35 amp), battery control	85 Switch, oil pressure
2 Inhibitor switch, automatic transmission	42 Switch, panel illumination	86 Switch, handbrake
3 Relay for starter motor	43 Screen wiper motor	87 Switch, brake fluid level
4 Battery	44 Fuse, 19–20 (15 amp), wiper motor	88 Stop light, RH
5 Thief-proof ignition coil	45 Switch, rheostat, screen wiper	89 Stop light, LH
6 Switch, ignition and starter	46 Relay, 3 AW, warning lights	90 Reverse light
7 Ammeter	47 Control, 4TR, alternator	91 Direction indicator, front, LH
8 Starter motor	48 Cigar lighter and switch	92 Repeater direction indicator, LH front
9 Distributor	49 Horns	93 Repeater direction indicator, LH rear
10 Side lamp, left-hand, RH Steering, right-hand LH Steering	50 Switch, screen wiper	94 Direction indicator, rear LH
	51 Warning light, ignition	95 Direction indicator, rear RH
11 Switch and lamp, boot	52 Relay, 6RA, alternator	96 Repeater direction indicator, RH rear
12 ⎱ Rear number plate	53 Alternator, 11 AC	97 Repeater direction indicator, RH front
13 ⎰ illumination	54 Interior lamp and switch, front, LH	98 Direction indicator, front RH
14 Tail lamp, left-hand, RH Steering, right-hand LH Steering	55 Switch, front door, LH	99 Switch, windscreen washer
	56 Interior lamp and switch, rear, LH	100 Windscreen washer
15 Headlamp, RH dip beam	57 Switch, rear door, LH	101 Water temperature gauge
16 Headlamp, LH dip beam	58 Interior lamp and switch, rear, RH	102 Water temperature transmitter
17 Headlamp, RH main beam	59 Switch, rear door, RH	103 Fuel tank unit
18 Headlamp, LH main beam	60 Interior lamp and switch, front, RH	104 Oil pressure gauge ⎫
19 Warning light, headlamp main beam	61 Switch, front door, RH	105 Oil pressure transmitter ⎪
20 Fog lamp, RH	62 Clock	106 To screen washer switch ⎪
21 Fog lamp, LH	63 Switch, horns	107 Tachometer ⎬ Coupé
22 Tail lamp (park) right-hand RH Steering, left-hand LH Steering	64 Clock illumination	108 Rear cigar lighter illumination ⎪
	65 Gear selector illumination	109 Cigar lighter ⎪
23 Side lamp (park) right-hand RH Steering, left-hand LH Steering	66 ⎱ Panel	110 Nacelle illumination, four lamps ⎭
	67 ⎰ illumination, RH	111 Switch, headrest lamp ⎫
24 Cigar lighter, front illumination	68 Grouped instrument illumination	112 Plug and socket, headrest lamp ⎪
25 ⎱ Panel	69 Fuse, 21–22 (15 amp), heater motor	113 Pick-up point when two lamps are fitted ⎪
26 ⎰ illumination, LH	70 Switch, heater, front	
27 Speedometer illumination	71 Heater illumination, rear	114 Headrest lamp ⎪
28 Switch, side-tail and park lamps	72 Switch, heater, rear	115 Switch, bonnet lamp* ⎪
29 Fuse, 7–8 (5 amp), side and tail lamps	73 Fuse, 3–4 (25 amp), ignition control	116 Bonnet lamp* ⎬ Optional
30 Fuse, 15–16 (10 amp), headlamp, RH dip	74 Warning light, brake fluid level and handbrake	117 Radio pick-up ⎪ equipment
31 Fuse, 17–18 (10 amp), headlamp, LH dip	75 Switch, stop light	118 Fuse, (25 amp) in-line, heated backlight ⎪
32 Fuse, 11–12 (15 amp), headlamp, RH main	76 Switch, reverse light	
33 Fuse, 13–14 (15 amp), headlamp, LH main	77 Warning light, LH direction indicators	119 Switch, illuminated, heated backlight ⎪
34 Switch, fog lamp	78 Direction indicator unit	120 Heated backlight ⎭
35 Fuse, 23–24 (25 amp), fog lamps	79 Warning light, RH direction indicators	121 Snap and Lucar connections
36 Switch, headlamp on steering column	80 Regulator, 10 volt	122 Fuses
37 Switch, headlamp dip	81 Fuel gauge	123 Earth connections
38 Switch, headlamp flasher	82 Heater motor, two-speed, front	
39 Fuse, 5–6 (5 amp), parking lights	83 Heater motor, two-speed, rear	*Standard on Coupé models
40 Fuse, 9–10 (5 amp), panel lights	84 Warning light, oil pressure	

Encircled letters on circuit diagram show pick-up points for additional and optional equipment

Cable colour code

B—Black   Y—Yellow   L—Light   P—Purple   N—Brown   K—Pink   W—White   U—Blue   S—Slate   R—Red   G—Green

The last letter of a colour code denotes the tracer colour

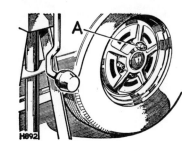

Wheel changing

A—Wheel nut

Wheel changing

1 Slacken the five wheel nuts.

2 Jack up the corner of the car. See page 42.

3 Remove the nuts and gently withdraw the wheel over the studs.

4 If available, place a drop of oil on the stud threads, to assist in subsequent removal.

5 Fit the wheel, tighten the nuts as much as possible, then lower the car to the ground and lock the nuts securely.

Body care

It is always preferable to clean the bodywork with water and sponge, using plenty of water; wherever possible the surface should be freely hosed. After drying with a chamois leather, it should be polished in the usual manner, using any of the good brands of wax car polish.

As an alternative, if the body is only dusty, it can be wiped over with a soft, dry cloth and then polished, but great care must be taken to avoid scratching the surface.

It is well periodically to wash the underside of the car, to prevent mud pockets and the consequent tendency for rust formation.

The use on the roads during frosty weather of salt, sometimes in quite strong concentrations, is now widely practised. Whilst special protection has been provided for the under surfaces of the body, etc., due to its highly corrosive nature, salt deposited should be washed off as soon as possible by thorough under-washing of the car.

Chromium cannot rust, but in instances where it is used on ferrous metals, it does not prevent the accumulation of red oxide on the chromium surface. Although continual polishing is not necessary, dirt must be removed periodically if the original high polish is to be maintained.

Ordinary metal polishes cannot be used, as some of them contain solutions which act as a solvent to chromium. The occasional use of a good brand of polish that has been specially prepared for chromium plate will be found useful.

The seats are trimmed with high-class leather free from any artificially embossed grain. Nature should show itself in every piece of high-class leather. The growth marks, vein marks and other natural marks and variations of grain that go to make up the character are the charm and hall-mark of top-grade leather. It is most important that detergents are not used when cleaning the seats, etc. Use a damp cloth with a little mild soap if necessary.

Layout of safety harness, right-hand side illustrated

A—Upper shoulder strap with quick-adjustment buckle
B—Quick-adjustment buckle
C—Lower shoulder strap with adaptor
D—'BC' post lower fixing and adjustment retaining bar
E—'BC' post upper fixing
F—Stowage hook for housing strap buckle
G—Housing strap with quick-adjustment buckle. This buckle should be as far round the body as possible without actually fouling the seat
H—Tunnel fixing for tongue strap

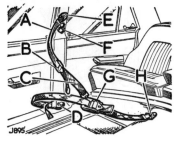

Upper shoulder strap with quick-adjustment buckle

A—Quick-adjustment buckle
B—Upper shoulder strap

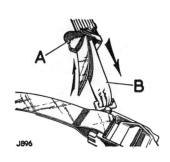

Safety harness—lift type release buckle illustrated

Safety harness must be fitted to the anchorage points provided at both the driver's and passengers' position to comply with legal requirements applicable in the United Kingdom.

Use only Rover-approved safety harness which is specially designed for the Rover 3½ litre.

The complete layout of the safety harness is shown in the adjacent illustration.

With the occupant seated in the front seat, the shoulder strap must pass over the outboard shoulder for both driver and passenger.

Before carrying out the initial adjustment at the 'BC' post lower position, seat position and seat rake must be correct for occupant. Then fully extend the quick-adjustment of upper shoulder strap at the buckle by lifting buckle and pulling strap in direction of arrow, as shown in illustration. Try the lap belt round the body for buckle position and make visual assessment of adjustment required. The buckle should be as far round the body as possible without actually fouling the seat.

To adjust the housing buckle, remove buckle by depressing pressure plate and pushing the buckle downwards in direction of arrow.

Push rubber protection sleeve to one side and release tension of strap retaining bar.

To shorten the housing strap, pull the upper strap. To lengthen the housing strap, pull the lower strap.

Do not lengthen the housing strap beyond the point where the loose end of the webbing is less than 25 mm (1 in.). When adjustment is correct, that is, the quick-release buckle is at the hip position, replace rubber protection sleeve, tuck loose end of strap into plastic sleeve and refit buckle to anchorage point.

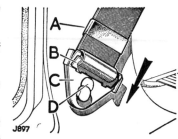

Housing strap buckle at lower 'BC' post

A—Rubber protection sleeve
B—Strap retaining bar
C—Buckle for housing strap
D—Pressure plate

Day-to-day use of safety harness

To attain the maximum designed protection from the safety harness, it is essential that it be properly fitted and adjusted. This can only be achieved by adhering to the following simple rules. It is most important to proceed in the order presented.

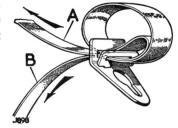

Adjustment of housing strap

A—Pull to shorten strap
B—Pull to lengthen strap

Fastening safety harness, stage 1

A—Buckle on upper shoulder strap

B—End of housing strap

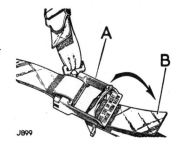

J899

Fastening safety harness, stage 2

A—Tongue on housing strap

B—End of housing strap

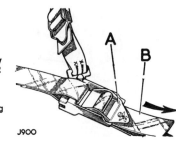

J900

With the occupant in the front seat, fasten the safety harness as follows:

(a) Slacken adjustment at quick-release buckle on shoulder strap.

(b) Hold buckle in one hand with the flat side to the body.

(c) Take the housing strap in the other hand, holding it so that the free end of seat strap is outward. The free end of the housing strap must not be passed through the buckle.

(d) Pass the tip of tongue through buckle and turn down the tongue in direction of arrow.

(e) Pull free end of housing strap in direction of arrow to adjust. Straps should be comfortably tight, just enough to allow the hand to be passed between upper shoulder strap and body.

(f) Then adjust quick-adjustment buckle on shoulder strap by pulling end of strap down.

To undo the buckle and leave the seat, simply lift the tip of the tongue. The two sections of the harness will instantly fall apart.

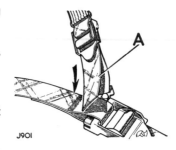

Adjustment of upper shoulder strap

A—End of lower shoulder strap

Seat belts which have been used in an accident or are frayed or cut must be replaced.

One of the objections to the use of seat harnesses, is the fact that they tend to become dirty. To overcome this, the seat harness fitted to your Rover 3½ litre can very easily be removed as follows:

(a) Depress pressure plate.

(b) Push harness lug so that the keyhole slot can be removed over the anchorage screw head.

(c) The safety harness may then be washed in hand-hot water with soap or household detergent. Do not use any other cleaning fluid.

To avoid soiling and twisting the safety harness when it is not in use the quick-release buckle should be stowed on the centre door pillar stowage hook.

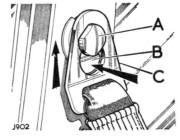

Safety harness removal

A—Anchorage screw head
B—Pressure plate
C—Harness lug

To refit the harness, align the large hole in the harness fixing lug with the anchorage screw head of the harness attachment, then push lug over screw head and compress pressure plate.

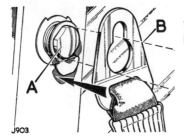

Refitting safety harness, stage 1

A—Anchorage screw head

B—Harness lug

Secure the harness lug to the anchorage by pulling to engage pressure plate in large hole of lug. Ensure that the spring-loaded plunger engages fully in the large hole.

Refitting safety harness, stage 2

Location of chassis serial number

The chassis number will be found on a plate affixed to the left-hand front door pillar. Always quote this number when writing to the Rover Company or your Distributor or Dealer on any matter concerning your car.

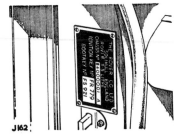

Chassis number

Location of engine serial number

The engine number is at the rear left of the engine adjacent to the back of the top rocker cover.

Do not quote this number unless requested.

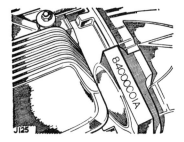

Engine number

PART THREE

GENERAL DATA, Saloon and Coupé models

Engine

Type	V8
Bore	88,90 mm (3.500 in.)
Stroke	71,12 mm (2.800 in.)
Number of cylinders	Eight
Cylinder capacity	3,528 cc (215 cu in.)
Compression ratio	10.5:1
BHP	184 (137 kw) at 5,200 rpm
Maximum torque	31 mkg (226 lb ft) at 3,000 rpm
Firing order	1, 8, 4, 3, 6, 5, 7, 2
Sparking plugs..	Champion L87Y. 14 mm with suppressed leads
Sparking plug point gap	0,60 mm (0.025 in.)
Distributor contact breaker gap	Dwell angle 26° – 28°. See also Distributor contact points—page 14
Ignition timing, dynamic setting at 500 to 600 rpm	6° BTDC mark on crankshaft pulley
Oil pressure	3,8 to 4,6 kg/cm² (30 to 40 lb/sq in.) at 80 kph (50 mph) in top gear with engine warm (2,400 rpm)
Lubrication	Full pressure
Oil filter—internal	Gauze pump intake filter in sump
Oil filter—external	Full-flow

Gearbox, automatic transmission

The automatic transmission consists of two main components:

1 A three-element hydrokinetic torque converter coupling capable of torque multiplication at an infinitely variable rate between 2.1:1 and 1:1.

2 A torque-speed responsive and hydraulically-operated gearbox comprising a planetary gear set providing three forward ratios and reverse.

Gear ratios

High (top)	**1.0:1**
Intermediate (2nd)	**1.45:1**
Low (1st)	**2.39:1**
Reverse	**2.09:1**

Propeller shafts

Type	Open type with centre bearing and support

Rear axle

Type	Spiral bevel with semi-floating shafts
Ratio	**3.54:1**

Fuel system

Fuel pump	A.C. mechanical, mounted on front left hand side of engine
Carburetter	Twin SU type HS6
Air cleaner	Twin paper element type

Cooling system

Type	Pump, fan and thermostat, pressurised to 1,0 kg/cm² (15 lb/sq in.)
Fan belt adjustment	11 to 14 mm (0.437 to 0.562 in.) free movement
Power steering pump belt adjustment	6 to 9 mm (0.25 to 0.375 in.) free movement

Suspension

Front	Laminated torsion bar
Rear	Progressive rate semi-elliptic leaf

Hydraulic dampers .. ..

Telescopic, anti-aeration, non-adjustable

Brakes

Foot brake	Hydraulic servo assisted, disc brakes at front, drum brakes at rear
Hand brake	Mechanical linkage to rear wheels

Steering

Type	Power assisted
Ratio: straight ahead	15.6:1
full lock	10.2:1
Front wheel alignment	1,5 mm (0.062 in.) toe-in to 1,5 mm (0.062 in.) toe-out

Camber angle	1.75°	⎫ Cars with	⎫
Castor angle	0.25° negative	⎬ Standard	Static
Swivel pin inclination..	4.25°	⎭ suspension	⎬ unladen
Camber angle	2°	⎫ Cars with High suspension	position
Castor angle	1° negative	⎬ marked H on serial	⎭
Swivel pin inclination..	4°	⎭ number plate	

Tyres

Size	Avon Turbospeed or Dunlop Roadspeed 6.70 in. x 15 in.				
Pressures:	Normal loads		Fully laden		
Speeds up to 168 kph (105 mph)	Front	Rear	Front	Rear	⎫
kg/cm^2	1,8	1,8	1,8	2,2	
lb/sq in.	26	26	26	32	
Bars	1.79	1.79	1.79	2.21	⎬ Check with
Speeds over 168 kph (105 mph)	Front	Rear	Front	Rear	tyres cold
kg/cm^2	2,1	2,1	2,1	2,4	
lb/sq in.	30	30	30	34	
Bars	2.07	2.07	2.07	2.34	⎭

When high speed touring, the tyre pressures should be checked much more frequently, even to the extent of a daily check.

Electrical system

Type	Negative earth
Voltage	12 volt ⎱ Battery located in luggage boot under metal cover
Battery capacity	57 AH ⎰ at right-hand rear
Ignition system	Coil
Charging circuit	Alternator with current-voltage regulator

Replacement headlamp units and bulbs

Headlamp units:

RHD	Lucas No. 59679 Sealed Beam 12v 75/50w
LHD except France	Lucas No. 410 12v 45/40w Duplo
LHD France	Lucas No. 411 12v 45/40w Duplo (yellow)
Side lamps and rear number plate lamp	Lucas No. 989 12v 6w
Stop/tail lamps..	Lucas No. 380 12v 21/6w
Direction indicator lamps and reverse lamp	Lucas No. 382 12v 21w
Fog lamp	Lucas No. 54522163 Sealed Beam 12v 50w
Cigar lighter illumination	Tex No. GBP-V-2.2 12v 2.2w
Speedometer and grouped instruments, tachometer on Coupé	Lucas No. 984 12v 3.6w
Warning lights, instrument panel lights and	
nacelle illumination	Lucas No. 987 12v 2.2w
Instrument panel switches	Lucas No. 981 12v 2w
Interior lights, festoon bulb	Lucas No. 254 12v 6w
Automatic transmission selector indicator lamp	Lucas No. 256 12v 3w
Panel plate	Carr Fastener No. 82/036 12v 1.2w
Clock and hand brake warning light	Lucas No. 281 12v 2w
Rear luggage boot lamp	Lucas No. 222 12v 4w
Bonnet lights, Coupé models	Tex SP No. 209 12v 6w

General data

Capacities

Component	Litres	Imperial unit	US unit
Engine sump oil	4,5	8 pints	9.6 pints
Extra when refilling after fitting new filter	0,5	1 pint	1.2 pints
Automatic transmission, with oil cooler	8,0	14 pints	17 pints
Rear axle oil	1,75	3 pints	3.5 pints
Power steering unit	1,75 to 1,8	3 to 3.5 pints	3.5 to 4 pints
Fuel tank	63,5	14 gallons	17 gallons
Including a reserve of	7	1.5 gallons	2 gallons
Cooling system	9,0	16 pints	19 pints

Dimensions—all models

Overall length .. .. 4,75 m (15 ft 7 in.)
Overall width .. .. 1,78 m (5 ft 10.5 in.)
Overall height, Saloon models .. .. Standard suspension 1,55 m (5 ft 1 in.)
High suspension* 1,56 m (5 ft 1.5 in.)
Overall height, Coupé models .. .. Standard suspension 1,46 m (4 ft 10 in.)
High suspension* 1,47 m (4 ft 10.5 in.)
Wheelbase .. .. 2,80 m (9 ft 2.5 in.)
Track, front .. .. 1,39 m (4 ft 7.312 in.)
Track, rear .. .. 1,41 m (4 ft 8 in.)
Ground clearance (under silencer) .. .. 180 mm (7.125 in.). 194 mm (7.625 in.) for high suspension
Turning circle between kerbs .. .. 12,2 m (40 ft), lock to lock 2.5 turns
*Identified by letter 'H' on car number plate affixed to left-hand front door pillar.

Weight, with water, oil and 22,5 litres (5 gallons) of fuel Saloon and Coupé 1.587 kg (3,500 lb)

Recommended lubricants and fluids

These recommendations apply to temperate climates where operational temperatures may vary between approximately −12°C (10°F) and 32°C (90°F).

Lubricants marked with an asterisk (*) are multigrade oils suitable for all temperature ranges.

Information on recommended lubricants for use under extreme winter or tropical conditions can be obtained from The Rover Co. Ltd, Technical Service Department, or your local Distributor or Dealer.

COMPONENTS	BP	CASTROL	DUCKHAM'S	ESSO	MOBIL	REGENT TEXACO/ CALTEX	SHELL
Engine	*BP Super Visco-Static 10W-40	*Castrol GTX	Duckham's Q20-50 Motor Oil	Uniflo or Esso Motor Oil 20W/50	Mobiloil Super	Havoline 20/20W	*Shell Super Oil
Automatic transmission and power steering	BP Autran B	Castrol TQF	Duckham's Q-Matic	Esso Glide	Mobil ATF 210	Texamatic Type F	Shell Donax T.7
Rear axle	BP Gear Oil SAE 90 EP	Castrol Hypoy	Duckham's Hypoid 90	Esso Gear Oil GX 90/140	Mobilube GX 90	Multigear Lubricant 90	Spirax 90 EP
Propeller shaft sliding spline, front hubs, rear spring and front torsion bar sleeves	BP Energrease L2	Castrol LM Grease	Duckham's LB10 Grease	Esso Multi-purpose Grease H	Mobilgrease MP or Mobilgrease Super	Marfak Multi-purpose	Retinax A or Darina AX
Brakes	Castrol Girling Brake and Clutch Fluid, Crimson, Specification J. 1703						
Anti-freeze solution for cooling system	Bluecol AA, coloured green, or any other anti-freeze solution conforming to British Standard No. 3150, or anti-freeze to MIL-E-5559 formulation. For summer and winter use						
Inhibitor solution for cooling system	Marston Lubricant SQ36—Coolant inhibitor concentrate. For summer use only if for any reason frost precautions are not required						

PART FOUR

FREE SERVICE AND MAINTENANCE SCHEDULES

The regular carrying out of the following schedules services is an extremely important factor in maintaining the value of the car and contributing to its reliability.

In addition to the regular maintenance schedules, details are also provided of the work to be done on the Free Service Inspection after the car has covered approximately its first 1.500 km (1,000 miles).

See Part One of this book for detailed information on the servicing required.

Provision has been made in this section for a certifying signature that the various services have been carried out so that there is a permanent record of these having been completed.

The word "check", where used, implies "rectify or investigate as necessary".

It will be noted that certain maintenance work which is required from time to time, but not necessarily at specified mileages, has been omitted from these schedules. This will include such work as decarbonising, brake pad and brake lining replacement, etc., the need for which will vary very much according to circumstances, and a Rover Distributor or Dealer should be consulted about such points at the time other service work is being carried out.

SUMMARY OF MAINTENANCE ATTENTION WHICH SHOULD BE CARRIED OUT AT OR AROUND SPECIFIED MILEAGES UP TO A TOTAL OF 64.000 KM (40,000 MILES)

IMPORTANT—ACTION BY OWNER

1 Every 1.000 km (750 miles) check engine oil level, power steering oil level, and water level in radiator and windscreen washer reservoir.

2 Drain and refill engine sump and change the oil filter every six months if mileage covered is less than 8.000 km (5,000 miles).

3 Every month check tyre pressures and inspect tyre treads; when high-speed touring the tyre pressures should be checked much more frequently, even to the extent of a daily check. If front wheel tread wear is uneven, check wheel alignment.

4 Every month check brake fluid level and battery acid level.

5 Owners are under a legal obligation to maintain all exterior lights in good working order, this also applies to headlamp beam setting, which should be checked at regular intervals. Distributor or Dealer Service.

6 When all the vouchers in this book have been completed owners are advised to apply to their Rover Distributor or Dealer for a copy of the Continuation Maintenance Schedule Book to enable the good work of preventive maintenance to be continued for another 64.000 km (40,000 miles).

7 It should be noted that the sequence of normal maintenance attention repeats itself every 32.000 km (20,000 miles).

AT 1.500 KM (1,000 MILES)

Free Service.

AT 8.000 KM (5,000 MILES)

Drain and refill engine sump (every 5,000 miles (8.000 km) or every six months, whichever comes first).

Renew external oil filter element.

Tune up engine as follows using electronic equipment

(a) Check dwell angle, 26°–28°
(b) Check ignition timing
(c) Check carburetter slow running ⎫ Engine at normal
(d) Check mixture setting ⎰ running temperature

Check and clean sparking plugs. Gap: 0,60 mm (0.025 in.).

Important—Use only Champion L87Y sparking plugs.

Check water level in screen washer reservoir (add Isopropyl alcohol in winter).

Check water level in radiator (anti-freeze).

Check fluid level in automatic transmission, top-up if necessary to 'full' mark on dipstick.

Check automatic transmission oil pressure. At 1,000 rpm, 6,3–7,3 kg/cm²(90–105 lb/sq in.).

Check differential oil level, top-up if necessary to bottom of filler plug hole.

Check fluid level in power steering reservoir, top-up if necessary to 'high' mark on dipstick.

Check fluid level in brake reservoir, top-up if necessary to rib on filter. Use Castrol Girling Crimson Brake and Clutch Fluid (Specification J. 1703).

Check operation of brake reservoir level safety switch.

Ignition 'on', hand brake 'off', unscrew and lift filler cap, 25 mm (1 in.); warning light should be illuminated.

AT 8.000 KM (5,000 MILES) cont.

Check thickness of front brake pads: minimum 3 mm (0.125 in.), also check for oil contamination on brake pads and discs.

Check and if necessary adjust rear wheel brakes. This automatically adjusts the hand brake.

Change round, wash and examine all road wheels for possible damage. Finally tighten all road wheel nuts.

Check tyre pressures. Normal motoring, front and rear: 1,8 kg/cm² (26 lb/sq in.), 1.79 Bars. Inspect tyre treads.

Lubricate propeller shaft sliding joint.

Check battery acid level and specific gravity of the electrolyte.

Road test, carry out any adjustments required. Check operation of fuel reserve control, run car for a short period with control out, finally push control in. Check operation of all lights and instruments. After test, check for oil, fuel or fluid leaks at all plugs, flanges, joints and unions. Check brake pipes and hoses for chafing and looseness. Report any defects.

Wipe clean all controls, handles, etc., clean windscreen and lights.

AT 16.000 KM (10,000 MILES)

As 8.000 km (5,000 miles) plus:

Replace air cleaner elements.

Check oil in carburetter hydraulic dampers.

Replace sparking plugs. Gap 0,60 mm (0.025 in.).

Important—Use only Champion L87Y sparking plugs.

Check distributor contact points. Dwell angle 26°—28°

Clean and lubricate distributor.

AT 16.000 KM (10,000 MILES) cont.

Check that rubber boots on steering ball joints and ball swivels are not dislodged or damaged.

Check fan and power steering pump belts. Fan belt 11 to 14 mm (0.437 to 0.562 in.) and power steering pump belt 6 to 9 mm (0.25 to 0.375 in.) free movement, when checked midway between pulleys.

Replace fuel filter.

Check front hubs for leakage.

Clean, grease and tighten battery terminals.

Check headlamp and fog lamp beam setting.

Apply a few spots of oil to throttle linkage, hand brake linkage, door locks, etc.

AT 24.000 KM (15,000 MILES)

As 8.000 km (5,000 miles).

AT 32.000 KM (20,000 MILES)

As 8.000 km (5,000 miles) and 16.000 km (10,000 miles) plus:

Clean flame traps.

Replace breather filter.

Drain and refill differential in place of checking oil level.

Check front wheel alignment 1,5 mm (0.062 in.) toe-in to 1,5 mm (0.062 in.) toe-out.

AT 40.000 KM (25,000 MILES)

As 8.000 km (5,000 miles).

SUMMARY OF MAINTENANCE ATTENTION—*continued*

AT 48.000 KM (30,000 MILES)

As 16.000 km (10,000 miles).

AT 56.000 KM (35,000 MILES)

As 8.000 km (5,000 miles).

AT 64.000 KM (40,000 MILES)

As 32.000 km (20,000 miles).

Clean filter in automatic enrichment device.

Renew all rubber seals and fluid in brake system. This should be done every three years if mileage covered is less than 64.000 km (40,000 miles). Refill with correct fluid. Castrol Girling Crimson Brake and Clutch Fluid (Specification J.1703).

NEW CAR PRE-DELIVERY CHECK

The Pre-delivery Check *must* be carried out in a thorough manner before the car is delivered to the owner.

The following sequence of operations under the headings of Engine Compartment, Interior and Boot, Underbody, Road Test and Final Preparation will enable this work to be carried out in the most efficient manner.

**NEW CAR
PRE-DELIVERY CHECK**

**Carried out by
Rover Distributor or
Dealer**

NAME.....................................

ADDRESS...............................

....

We certify that the New Car Pre-delivery Check has been completed

Signature...............................

Date..

ENGINE COMPARTMENT—vehicle on a level floor

1 Check engine automatic transmission and power steering reservoir oil levels
2 Check coolant level in radiator (anti-freeze specific gravity in winter), and drain taps for leakage
3 Fill windscreen washer reservoir, using the additive supplied (methylated spirits in winter)
4 Check brake reservoir fluid level—test fluid level warning light by switching on ignition, unscrewing and raising reservoir cap approximately one inch (25 mm), and ensuring warning light is illuminated with the hand brake in the 'off' position
5 Check all joints, pipes, flanges and hoses for oil, fluid or coolant leakage
6 Check tension of both auxiliary drive belts; refer to Part One of this book for adjustment details, if required
7 Check for security of attachment all electrical connections (alternator, starter, voltage regulator, fuse box, solenoid and coil, distributor low tension lead, high tension leads and spark plug connections, oil pressure and engine temperature transmitters, etc.)
8 Check the distributor vacuum pipe for leaks
9 Close bonnet and check lock and safety catch

INTERIOR AND BOOT—vehicle on a level floor

10 Check the operation of all door locks and courtesy lighting
11 Check operation of all window regulators and vent window locking mechanisms
12 Check operation of glove box fasteners and locks
13 Check operation of time clock and reset as necessary

14 Check for correct operation adjustment mechanisms and security of front seats. Check adjustable armrests
15 Ensure that tool tray carries the full tool kit
16 With ignition switched on, check operation of the following instruments and controls:
 (a) Hand brake operation and warning light, stop lamp and reverse lamp
 (b) Fuel gauge, ignition and oil warning lights
 (c) Side, parking and headlamp switches, instrument lighting and rheostat control. Check gear selector quadrant illumination
 (d) Operate dip switch, and check functioning of main beam warning light
 (e) Switch off head and side lamps. Check operation of direction flashers and headlamp flasher switch and corresponding warning lights
 (f) Check operation of horn ring and horns
 (g) Windscreen wipers and rheostat control
 (h) Windscreen washers, ensuring that both jets are correctly positioned
 (j) Interior lighting switches, cigar lighters, clock and rear window demister, when fitted. Switch off ignition
17 Check the operation of boot catch, lock and illumination lamp
18 Check the battery acid level and specific gravity of the electrolyte. Also battery post terminals for security.
19 Check tools for correct stowage and deficiencies

CONTINUED OVERLEAF

NEW CAR PRE-DELIVERY CHECK

20 Check spare wheel is correctly inflated and stowed

21 Close boot lid

22 Check all tyre pressures and wheel nuts, ensuring that valve caps are carefully replaced

UNDERBODY—vehicle on ramp

23 Place car on ramp or over pit

24 Check drain taps for leakage

25 Check exhaust pipe and silencer mountings for security

26 Check engine sump, automatic transmission and rear axle for oil leakage

27 Check rear axle differential oil level

28 Carry out an underbody inspection, checking for any irregularities, including hydraulic leaks

ROAD TEST

29 Carry out a short but careful road test after checking for correct operation of ignition and oil pressure warning lights, and on Coupé models the tachometer, oil pressure gauge and ammeter

30 During test pay particular attention to behaviour of engine, torque converter, automatic transmission control linkage, brakes (foot and hand) and the steering mechanism. Check for body noises

31 Check operation of speedometer, mileage and trip recorder, correct positioning of steering wheel. Check operation of engine temperature gauge

32 With engine at normal running temperature, carry out the following checks:

(a) The choke warning light (momentarily) and fast-idle control

(b) The operation of fuel reserve control, allowing the engine to run for a short time with the control in both positions

(c) Check for correct functioning of the heater controls; that is, temperature control, distribution control and two-speed fan control, front and rear

FINAL PREPARATION

33 Wash car and ensure interior cleanliness, checking for damaged trim or carpets

34 Carefully examine the car exterior for damage and security and finish of chrome and stainless steel parts

35 Check all glass sections for scratches or other blemishes

36 Make sure the owner is conversant with all controls and, if necessary, accompany him on a short instruction run.

37 Check that all literature is complete

FREE SERVICE AT 1.500 KM (1,000 MILES)

For recommended lubricants and capacities see Part Three of this book, pages 60 and 61

Lubricants and materials are chargeable

Carried out by
Rover Distributor or
Dealer

Owner's signature..giving authority for the work detailed below to be carried out

Special attention should be given to any complaint by the owner

NAME..

ADDRESS....................................

....

We certify that the
Free Service has been
completed

Signature......................................

Mileage...

Km...

Date..

Engine

Note and report any oil leakage for rectification action

Drain and refill engine sump

Check carburetter slow-running at normal running temperature

Check oil in carburetter hydraulic dampers

Check and if necessary clean sparking plugs. Gap .025 in. (0,60 mm)

Check distributor contact points. Dwell angle 26°—28°

Lubricate and clean distributor

Check water level in radiator (anti-freeze)

Check water level in screen washer reservoir (add methylated spirits in winter)

Check fan and power steering pump belts. fan belt $\frac{7}{16}$ to $\frac{9}{16}$ in. (11 to 14 mm) and power steering belt $\frac{1}{4}$ to $\frac{3}{8}$ in. (6 to 9 mm) free movement when checked midway between pulleys

Lubricate accelerator linkage and check for correct operation

Check security of alternator, power steering pump and exhaust manifold fixings

Check all visible wiring for damage and connections for security

Automatic transmission

Note and report any oil leakage for rectification action

The automatic gearbox level should be checked with engine idling and 'Park' selected

Check fluid level, top-up if necessary to 'full' mark on dipstick

Rear axle

Note and report any oil leakage for rectification action

Drain and refill differential

Steering and suspension

Note and report any oil leakage for rectification action

Check oil level in power steering reservoir, top-up if necessary to 'high' mark on dipstick

Check that rubber boots on steering ball joints and ball swivels are not dislodged or damaged

Check front hubs for leakage

Leakage from front hubs may indicate that the hubs have insufficient clearance causing overheating. See Workshop Manual for setting details

Check front wheel alignment. $\frac{1}{16}$ in. (1,5 mm) toe-in to $\frac{1}{16}$ in. (1,5 mm) toe-out

Check that rear spring gaiters are not dislodged or damaged

Inspect shock absorbers for security of attachment

Brakes

Check fluid level in reservoir, top-up if necessary to rib on filter, use Girling Crimson Brake Fluid (Specification SAE 70R3)

Check operation of reservoir level safety switch. Ignition 'on', hand brake 'off', unscrew and lift filler cap 1 in. (25 mm); light should be illuminated

CONTINUED OVERLEAF

Check operation of hand brake linkage and lubricate if necessary

Check front pads and discs, rear shoes and drums for any signs of oil contamination

Carefully inspect all pipes, hoses and unions for leakage or signs of chafing

Fuel system

Check pipes and unions for leakage and security

Wheels and tyres

Check tyre pressures and inspect tyre treads and walls for damage. Front and rear: 26 lb/sq in. (1,8 kg/cm²)

Check tightness of wheel nuts

Propeller shafts

Lubricate sliding joint

Check securing bolts

Electrical

Check battery acid level and specific gravity of the electrolyte

Check battery terminals for cleanliness and security

Inspect all visible wiring for damage or loose connections

Check all circuits and instruments for correct operation

Road test

Give car a thorough road test and carry out any adjustments required

During test check operation of brake servo unit

Run car with reserve fuel control out for a short period to ensure that the control operates correctly. Push control in

Check operation of all lights and instruments

After test, check for oil, fuel, fluid or grease leaks at all plugs, flanges, joints and unions

Report any defects

Body

Check all fasteners, locks, window controls, etc. for correct operation. Rectify as necessary

Cleaning

Wash car and wipe clean all controls, handles, etc., clean windscreen and lights

Inspect paintwork and chromium plating for defects and blemishes

For recommended lubricants and capacities see Part Three of this book, pages 60 and 61

Owner's signature..giving authority for the work detailed below to be carried out

MAINTENANCE ATTENTION AT 8.000 KM (5,000 MILES)

Carried out by Rover Distributor or Dealer

NAME..

ADDRESS................................

....

We certify that the 8.000 km (5,000-mile) maintenance attention has been completed

Signature.......................................

Km...

Mileage..

Date..

Engine

Note and report any oil leakage for rectification action

Drain and refill engine sump

Renew external oil filter element

Tune up engine as follows using electronic equipment

(a) Check dwell angle, 26°–28°

(b) Check ignition timing. Dynamic setting, 6° BTDC at 500–600 rpm

(c) Check carburetter slow-running ⎫ Engine at normal
(d) Check mixture setting ⎭ running temperature

Check and clean sparking plugs. Gap 0,60 mm (0.025 in.)· *Important*—Use only Champion L87Y sparking plugs

Check water level in screen washer reservoir (add Isopropyl alcohol in winter)

Check water level in radiator (anti-freeze)

Automatic transmission

Note and report any oil leakage for rectification action

The automatic gearbox level should be checked with engine idling and 'Park' selected

Check fluid level, top-up if necessary to 'full' mark on dipstick

Check oil pressure in automatic transmission:

(a) Chock front wheels and apply handbrake firmly
Apply foot brake during test

(b) Connect pressure gauge and tachometer

(c) Start the engine and allow to warm up

(d) Move selector lever to 'D' or '2' position. ('D2' or 'D1' on early models)

(e) The pressures should be:
At 1,000 rpm 90-105 lb/sq in. (6,3-7,3 kg/cm^2)

(f) If pressure is more than 105 lb/sq in. (7,3 kg/cm^2) screw in downshift cable adjuster

Rear axle

Note and report any oil leakage for rectification action

Check differential oil level, top-up if necessary to bottom of filler plug hole

Steering and suspension

Note and report any oil leakage for rectification action

Check fluid level in power steering reservoir, top-up if necessary to 'high' mark on dipstick

Brakes. See also Road Test

Check fluid level in reservoir, top-up if necessary to rib on filter. Use Girling Crimson Brake Fluid (Specification J. 1703)

Check operation of reservoir level safety switch. Ignition 'on'· hand brake 'off', unscrew and lift filler cap 25 mm (1 in.); warning light should be illuminated

Check thickness of front brake pads, minimum 3 mm (0.125 in.) also check for oil contamination on brake pads and discs

Check and if necessary adjust rear wheel brakes. This automatically adjusts the hand brake

Change fluid in brake system every eighteen months

CONTINUED OVERLEAF

Wheels and tyres

Change round, wash and examine all road wheels for possible damage. Finally tighten all road wheel nuts

Check tyre pressures and inspect tyre treads and side walls for possible damage. Minimum tread depth 1 mm. Pressures: Front and rear: 1,8 kg/cm² (26 lb/sq in.), 1.79 bars.

Propeller shaft

Lubricate sliding joint

Electrical

Check battery acid level and specific gravity of the electrolyte

Road test

Give car a thorough road test and carry out any adjustments required. Run car with reserve fuel control out for a short period to ensure that the control operates correctly. Push control in

Check operation of all lights and instruments

After test, check for oil, fuel, fluid or grease leaks at all plugs, flanges, joints and unions. Check all brake pipes and hoses for chafing or looseness

Report any defects

Cleaning

Wipe clean all controls, handles, etc., clean windscreen and lights

**MAINTENANCE
ATTENTION AT
16.000 KM (10,000 MILES)**

For recommended lubricants and capacities see Part Three of this book, pages 60 and 61

**Carried out by
Rover Distributor or
Dealer**

Owner's signature..giving authority for the work detailed below to be carried out

NAME...

ADDRESS...................................

....

We certify that the 16.000 km
(10,000-mile) maintenance
attention has been completed

Signature....................................

Km...

Mileage...

Date..

Engine

Note and report any oil leakage for rectification action
Drain and refill engine sump
Renew external oil filter element
Replace air cleaner elements
Tune up engine as follows using electronic equipment
(a) Check dwell angle, 26°–28°
(b) Check ignition timing. Dynamic setting, 6° BTDC at 500–600 rpm
(c) Check carburetter slow-running ⎫ Engine at normal
(d) Check mixture setting ⎰ running temperature
Check oil in carburetter hydraulic dampers
Replace fuel filter
Replace sparking plugs. Gap 0,60 mm (0.025 in.)
Important—Use only Champion L87Y sparking plugs
Check distributor contact points. Dwell angle 26°—28°
Lubricate and clean distributor
Check water level in screen washer reservoir (add Isopropyl alcohol in winter)
Check water level in radiator (anti-freeze)
Check fan and power steering pump belts. Fan belt 11 to 14 mm (0.437 to 0.562 in.) and power steering belt 6 to 9 mm (0.25 to 0.375 in.) free movement when checked midway between pulleys

Automatic transmission

Note and report any oil leakage for rectification action
The automatic gearbox level should be checked with engine idling and 'Park' selected
Check fluid level, top-up if necessary to 'full' mark on dipstick

Check oil pressure in automatic transmission:
(a) Chock front wheels and apply handbrake firmly Apply foot brake during test
(b) Connect pressure gauge and tachometer
(c) Start the engine and allow to warm up
(d) Move selector lever to 'D' or '2' position. ('D2' or 'D1' on early models)
(e) The pressures should be: At 1,000 rpm 90-105 lb/sq in. (6,3-7,3 kg/cm²)
(f) If pressure is more than 105 lb/sq in. (7,3 kg/cm²) screw in downshift cable adjuster

Rear axle

Note and report any oil leakage for rectification action
Check differential oil level, top-up if necessary to bottom of filler plug hole

Steering and suspension

Note and report any oil leakage for rectification action
Check fluid level in power steering reservoir, top-up if necessary to 'high' mark on dipstick
Check that rubber boots on steering ball joints and ball swivels are not dislodged or damaged
Check front hubs for leakage

CONTINUED OVERLEAF

Brakes. See also Road Test

Check fluid level in reservoir, top-up if necessary to rib on filter. Use Girling Crimson Brake Fluid (Specification J.1703)

Check operation of reservoir level safety switch. Ignition 'on', hand brake 'off', unscrew and lift filler cap 25 mm (1 in.); warning light should be illuminated

Check thickness of front brake pads, minimum 0.125 (3mm) also check for oil contamination on brake pads and discs

Check and if necessary adjust rear wheel brakes. This automatically adjusts the hand brake

Change fluid in brake system every eighteen months

Wheels and tyres

Change round, wash and examine all road wheels for possible damage. Finally tighten all road wheel nuts

Check tyre pressures and inspect tyre treads and side walls for possible damage. Minimum tread depth 1 mm. Pressures: Front and rear: 1,8 kg/cm² (26 lb/sq in.), 1.79 bars

Propeller shaft

Lubricate sliding joint

Electrical

Check battery acid level and specific gravity of the electrolyte

Clean, grease and tighten battery terminals

Check headlamp and fog lamp beam setting

Oil can lubrication

Apply a few spots of oil to throttle linkage, hand brake linkage, door locks, etc.

Road test

Give car a thorough road test and carry out any adjustments required. Run car with reserve fuel control out for a short period to ensure that the control operates correctly. Push control in

Check operation of all lights and instruments

After test, check for oil, fuel, fluid or grease leaks at all plugs, flanges, joints and unions. Check all brake pipes and hoses for chafing or looseness

Report any defects

Cleaning

Wipe clean all controls, handles, etc., clean windscreen and lights

MAINTENANCE ATTENTION AT 24.000 KM (15,000 MILES)

For recommended lubricants and capacities see Part Three of this book, pages 60 and 61

Owner's signature...giving authority for the work detailed below to be carried out

**Carried out by
Rover Distributor or
Dealer**

NAME..

ADDRESS..................................

....

We certify that the 24.000 km
(15,000-mile) maintenance
attention has been completed

Signature....................................

Km..

Mileage.......................................

Date..

Engine

Note and report any oil leakage for rectification action

Drain and refill engine sump

Renew external oil filter element

Tune up engine as follows using electronic equipment

(a) Check dwell angle, 26°–28°

(b) Check ignition timing. Dynamic setting, 6° BTDC at 500–600 rpm

(c) Check carburetter slow-running } Engine at normal
(d) Check mixture setting } running temperature

Check and clean sparking plugs. Gap 0,60 mm (0.025 in.).
Important—Use only Champion L87Y sparking plugs

Check water level in screen washer reservoir (add Isopropyl alcohol in winter)

Check water level in radiator (anti-freeze)

Automatic transmission

Note and report any oil leakage for rectification action

The automatic gearbox level should be checked with engine idling and 'Park' selected

Check fluid level, top-up if necessary to 'full' mark on dipstick

Check oil pressure in automatic transmission:

(a) Chock front wheels and apply handbrake firmly
Apply foot brake during test

(b) Connect pressure gauge and tachometer

(c) Start the engine and allow to warm up

(d) Move selector lever to 'D' or '2' position.   ('D2' or 'D1' on early models)

(e) The pressures should be:
At 1,000 rpm 90-105 lb/sq in. (6,3-7,3 kg/cm^2)

(f) If pressure is more than 105 lb/sq in. (7,3 kg/cm^2) screw in downshift cable adjuster

Rear axle

Note and report any oil leakage for rectification action

Check differential oil level, top-up if necessary to bottom of filler plug hole

Steering and suspension

Note and report any oil leakage for rectification action

Check fluid level in power steering reservoir, top-up if necessary to 'high' mark on dipstick

Brakes. See also Road Test

Check fluid level in reservoir, top-up if necessary to rib on filter. Use Girling Crimson Brake Fluid (Specification J. 1703)

Check operation of reservoir level safety switch. Ignition 'on', hand brake 'off', unscrew and lift filler cap 25 mm (1 in.); warning light should be illuminated

Check thickness of front brake pads, minimum 3 mm (0.125 in.); also check for oil contamination on brake pads and discs

Check and if necessary adjust rear wheel brakes. This automatically adjusts the hand brake

Change fluid in brake system every eighteen months

CONTINUED OVERLEAF

Wheels and tyres

Change round, wash and examine all road wheels for possible damage. Finally tighten all road wheel nuts

Check tyre pressures and inspect tyre treads and side walls for possible damage. Minimum tread depth 1 mm. Pressures: Front and rear: 1,8 kg/cm2 (26 lb/sq in.), 1.79 bars

Propeller shaft

Lubricate sliding joint

Electrical

Check battery acid level and specific gravity of the electrolyte

Road test

Give car a thorough road test and carry out any adjustments required. Run car with reserve fuel control out for a short period to ensure that the control operates correctly. Push control in

Check operation of all lights and instruments

After test, check for oil, fuel, fluid or grease leaks at all plugs, flanges, joints and unions. Check all brake pipes and hoses for chafing or looseness

Report any defects

Cleaning

Wipe clean all controls, handles, etc., clean windscreen and lights

MAINTENANCE ATTENTION AT 32.000 KM (20,000 MILES)

For recommended lubricants and capacities see Part Three of this book, pages 60 and 61

Owner's signature...giving authority for the work detailed below to be carried out

Carried out by
Rover Distributor or
Dealer

NAME..

ADDRESS..................................

....

We certify that the 32.000 km
(20,000-mile) maintenance
attention has been completed

Signature......................................

Km ....

Mileage...

Date ....

Engine

Note and report any oil leakage for rectification action
Drain and refill engine sump
Renew external oil filter element
Tune up engine as follows using electronic equipment
(a) Check dwell angle, 26°–28°
(b) Check ignition timing. Dynamic setting, 6° BTDC at 500–600 rpm
(c) Check carburetter slow-running ⎫ Engine at normal
(d) Check mixture setting ⎭ running temperature
Check oil in carburetter hydraulic dampers
Replace air cleaner elements
Replace fuel filter
Replace breather filter
Clean flame traps
Replace sparking plugs. Gap: 0,60 mm (0.025 in.)
Important—Use only Champion L87Y sparking plugs
Check distributor contact points. Dwell angle 26°–28°
Lubricate and clean distributor
Check water level in screen washer reservoir (add Isopropyl alcohol in winter)
Check water level in radiator (anti-freeze)
Check fan and power steering pump belts. fan belt 11 to 14 mm (0.437 to 0.562 in.) and power steering belt 6 to 9 mm (0.25 to 0.375 in.) free movement when checked midway between pulleys

Automatic transmission

Note and report any oil leakage for rectification action
The automatic gearbox level should be checked with engine idling and 'Park' selected
Check fluid level, top-up if necessary to 'full' mark on dipstick

Check oil pressure in automatic transmission:
(a) Chock front wheels and apply handbrake firmly Apply foot brake during test
(b) Connect pressure gauge and tachometer
(c) Start the engine and allow to warm up
(d) Move selector lever to 'D' or '2' position. ('D2' or 'D1' on early models)
(e) The pressures should be:
At 1,000 rpm 90-105 lb/sq in. (6,3-7,3 kg/cm^2)
(f) If pressure is more than 105 lb/sq in. (7,3 kg/cm^2) screw in downshift cable adjuster

Rear axle

Note and report any oil leakage for rectification action
Drain and refill differential

Steering and suspension

Note and report any oil leakage for rectification action
Check fluid level in power steering reservoir, top-up if necessary to 'high' mark on dipstick
Check that rubber boots on steering ball joints and ball swivels are not dislodged or damaged
Check front hubs for leakage
Check front wheel alignment:
1,5 mm (0.062 in.) toe-in to 1,5 mm (0.062 in.) toe-out

CONTINUED OVERLEAF

Brakes. See also Road Test

Check fluid level in reservoir, top-up if necessary to rib on filter. Use Girling Crimson Brake Fluid (Specification J.1703)

Check operation of reservoir level safety switch. Ignition 'on', hand brake 'off', unscrew and lift filler cap 25 mm (1 in.); warning light should be illuminated

Check thickness of front brake pads, minimum 3 mm (0.125 in.), also check for oil contamination on brake pads and discs

Check and if necessary adjust rear wheel brakes. This automatically adjusts the hand brake

Replace brake servo filter

Change fluid in brake system every eighteen months

Wheels and tyres

Change round, wash and examine all road wheels for possible damage. Finally tighten all road wheel nuts

Check tyre pressures and inspect tyre treads and side walls for possible damage. Minimum tread depth 1 mm. Pressures: Front and rear: 1,8 kg/cm^2 (26 lb/sq in.), 1.79 bars

Propeller shaft

Lubricate sliding joint

Electrical

Check battery acid level and specific gravity of the electrolyte

Clean, grease and tighten battery terminals

Check headlamp and fog lamp beam setting

Oil can lubrication

Apply a few spots of oil to throttle linkage, hand brake linkage door locks, etc.

Road test

Give car a thorough road test and carry out any adjustments required

Run car with reserve fuel control out for a short period to ensure that the control operates correctly. Push control in

Check operation of all lights and instruments

After test, check for oil, fuel, fluid, or grease leaks at all plugs, flanges, joints and unions. Check all brake pipes and hoses for chafing or looseness

Report any defects

Cleaning

Wipe clean all controls, handles, etc., clean windscreen and lights

MAINTENANCE ATTENTION AT 40.000 KM (25,000 MILES)

MAINTENANCE
ATTENTION AT
56.000 KM (35,000 MILES)

Carried out by
Rover Distributor or
Dealer

NAME............................

ADDRESS...........................

....

We certify that the 56.000 km
(35,000-mile) maintenance
attention has been completed

Signature...............................

Km....................................

Mileage.............................

Date...............................

For recommended lubricants and capacities see Part Three of this book, pages 60 and 61

Owner's signature...giving authority for the work detailed below to be carried out

Engine

Note and report any oil leakage for rectification action
Drain and refill engine sump
Renew external oil filter element
Tune up engine as follows using electronic equipment

(a) Check dwell angle, 26°–28°
(b) Check ignition timing. Dynamic setting, 6° BTDC at 500–600 rpm
(c) Check carburetter slow-running ⎫ Engine at normal
(d) Check mixture setting ⎭ running temperature

Check and clean sparking plugs. Gap: 0.60 mm (0.025 in.).
Important—Use only Champion L87Y sparking plugs
Check water level in screen washer reservoir (add Isopropyl alcohol in winter)
Check water level in radiator (anti-freeze)

Automatic transmission

Note and report any oil leakage for rectification action
The automatic gearbox level should be checked with engine idling and 'Park' selected
Check fluid level, top-up if necessary to 'full' mark on dipstick
Check oil pressure in automatic transmission

(a) Chock front wheels and apply handbrake firmly
    Apply foot brake during test
(b) Connect pressure gauge and tachometer
(c) Start the engine and allow to warm up
(d) Move selector lever to 'D' or '2' position. ('D2' or 'D1' on early models)

(e) The pressures should be:
    At 1,000 rpm 90-105 lb/sq in. (6,3-7,3 kg/cm^2)
(f) If pressure is more than 105lb /sq in. (7,3 kg/cm^2) screw in downshift cable adjuster

Rear axle

Note and report any oil leakage for rectification action
Check differential oil level, top-up if necessary to bottom of filler plug hole

Steering and suspension

Note and report any oil leakage for rectification action
Check fluid level in power steering reservoir, top-up if necessary to 'high' mark on dipstick

Brakes. See also Road Test

Check fluid level in reservoir, top-up if necessary to rib on filter. Use Girling Crimson Brake Fluid (Specification J. 1703)
Check operation of reservoir level safety switch. Ignition 'on', hand brake 'off', unscrew and lift filler cap 25 mm (1 in.); warning light should be illuminated
Check thickness of front brake pads, minimum 3 mm (0.125 in.), also check for oil contamination on brake pads and discs
Check and if necessary adjust rear wheel brakes. This automatically adjusts the hand brake
Change fluid in brake system every eighteen months

CONTINUED OVERLEAF

MAINTENANCE ATTENTION AT 40.000 KM (25,000 MILES)

83

Wheels and tyres

Change round, wash and examine all road wheels for possible damage. Finally tighten all road wheel nuts

Check tyre pressures and inspect tyre treads and side walls for possible damage. Minimum tread depth 1 mm. Pressures: Front and rear: 1,8 kg/cm^2 (26 lb/sq in.), 1.79 bars

Propeller shaft

Lubricate sliding joint

Electrical

Check battery acid level and specific gravity of the electrolyte

Road test

Give car a thorough road test and carry out any adjustments required

Run car with reserve fuel control out for a short period to ensure that the control operates correctly. Push control in

Check operation of all lights and instruments

After test, check for oil, fuel, fluid or grease leaks at all plugs, flanges, joints and unions. Check all brake pipes and hoses for chafing or looseness

Report any defects

Cleaning

Wipe clean all controls, handles, etc., clean windscreen and lights

For recommended lubricants and capacities see Part Three of this book, pages 60 and 61

Owner's signature..giving authority for the work detailed below to be carried out

**Carried out by
Rover Distributor or
Dealer**

NAME...

ADDRESS...................................

....

We certify that the 48.000 km
(30,000-mile) maintenance
attention has been completed

Signature.......................................

Km....................................

Mileage ....

Date.--------------------------------

Engine

Note and report any oil leakage for rectification action

Drain and refill engine sump

Renew external oil filter element

Replace air cleaner elements

Tune up engine as follows using electronic equipment

(a) Check dwell angle, 26°–28°

(b) Check ignition timing. Dynamic setting, 6° BTDC at 500–600 rpm

(c) Check carburetter slow-running ⎫ Engine at normal

(d) Check mixture setting ⎭ running temperature

Check oil in carburetter hydraulic dampers

Replace fuel filter

Replace sparking plugs. Gap: 0,60 mm (0.025 in.)

Important—Use only Champion L87Y sparking plugs

Check distributor contact points. Dwell angle 26°—28°

Lubricate and clean distributor

Check water level in screen washer reservoir (add Isopropyl alcohol in winter)

Check water level in radiator (anti-freeze)

Check fan and power steering pump belts. Fan belt 11 to 14 mm (0.437 to 0.562 in.) and power steering belt 6 to 9 mm (0.25 to 0.375 in.) free movement when checked midway between pulleys

Automatic transmission

Note and report any oil leakage for rectification action

The automatic gearbox level should be checked with engine idling and 'Park' selected

Check fluid level, top-up if necessary to 'full' mark on dipstick

Check oil pressure in automatic transmission:

(a) Chock front wheels and apply handbrake firmly Apply foot brake during test

(b) Connect pressure gauge and tachometer

(c) Start the engine and allow to warm up

(d) Move selector lever to 'D' or '2' position. ('D2' or 'D1' on early models)

(e) The pressures should be:
At 1,000 rpm 90-105 lb/sq in. (6,3-7,3 kg/cm^2)

(f) If pressure is more than 105 lb/sq in. (7,3 kg/cm^2) screw in downshift cable adjuster

Rear axle

Note and report any oil leakage for rectification action

Check differential oil level, top-up if necessary to bottom of filler plug hole

Steering and suspension

Note and report any oil leakage for rectification action

Check fluid level in power steering reservoir, top-up if necessary to 'high' mark on dipstick

Check that rubber boots on steering ball joints and ball swivels are not dislodged or damaged

Check front hubs for leakage

CONTINUED OVERLEAF

Brakes. See also Road Test

Check fluid level in reservoir, top-up if necessary to rib on filter. Use Girling Crimson Brake Fluid (Specification J. 1703)

Check operation of reservoir level safety switch. Ignition 'on', hand brake 'off', unscrew and lift filler cap 25 mm (1 in.); warning light should be illuminated

Check thickness of front brake pads, minimum 3 mm (0.125 in.), also check for oil contaimination on brake pads and discs

Check and if necessary adjust rear wheel brakes. This automatically adjusts the hand brake

Change fluid in brake system every eighteen months

Wheels and tyres

Change round, wash and examine all road wheels for possible damage. Finally tighten all road wheel nuts

Check tyre pressures and inspect tyre treads and side walls for possible damage. Minimum tread depth 1 mm. Pressures: Front and rear: 1,8 kg/cm^2 (26 lb/sq in.), 1.79 bars

Propeller shaft

Lubricate sliding joint

Electrical

Check battery acid level and specific gravity of the electrolyte

Clean, grease and tighten battery terminals

Check headlamp beam setting

Oil can lubrication

Apply a few spots of oil to throttle linkage, hand brake linkage, door locks, etc.

Road test

Give car a thorough road test and carry out any adjustments required

Run car with reserve fuel control out for a short period to ensure that the control operates correctly. Push control in

Check operation of all lights and instruments

After test, check for oil, fuel, fluid or grease leaks at all plugs, flanges, joints and unions. Check all brake pipes and hoses for chafing or looseness

Report any defects

Cleaning

Wipe clean all controls, handles, etc., clean windscreen and lights

For recommended lubricants and capacities see Part Three of this book, pages 60 and 61

**Carried out by
Rover Distributor or
Dealer**

Owner's signature..giving authority for the work detailed below to be carried out

NAME......... ....

ADDRESS.................................

....

We certify that the 56.000 km
(35,000-mile) maintenance
attention has been completed

Signature.......................................

Km... ....

Mileage...

Date.................. ....

Engine

Note and report any oil leakage for rectification action

Drain and refill engine sump

Renew external oil filter element

Tune up engine as follows using electronic equipment

(a) Check dwell angle, 26°–28°

(b) Check ignition timing. Dynamic setting, 6° BTDC at 500–600 rpm

(c) Check carburetter slow-running ⎱ Engine at normal
(d) Check mixture setting ⎰ running temperature

Check and clean sparking plugs. Gap: 0.60 mm (0.025 in.)·
Important—Use only Champion L87Y sparking plugs

Check water level in screen washer reservoir (add Isopropyl alcohol in winter)

Check water level in radiator (anti-freeze)

Automatic transmission

Note and report any oil leakage for rectification action

The automatic gearbox level should be checked with engine idling and 'Park' selected

Check fluid level, top-up if necessary to 'full' mark on dipstick

Check oil pressure in automatic transmission

(a) Chock front wheels and apply handbrake firmly
Apply foot brake during test

(b) Connect pressure gauge and tachometer

(c) Start the engine and allow to warm up

(d) Move selector lever to 'D' or '2' position.   ('D2' or 'D1' on early models)

(e) The pressures should be:
At 1,000 rpm 90-105 lb/sq in. (6,3-7,3 kg/cm²)

(f) If pressure is more than 105lb /sq in. (7,3 kg/cm²) screw in downshift cable adjuster

Rear axle

Note and report any oil leakage for rectification action

Check differential oil level, top-up if necessary to bottom of filler plug hole

Steering and suspension

Note and report any oil leakage for rectification action

Check fluid level in power steering reservoir, top-up if necessary to 'high' mark on dipstick

Brakes. See also Road Test

Check fluid level in reservoir, top-up if necessary to rib on filter. Use Girling Crimson Brake Fluid (Specification J. 1703)

Check operation of reservoir level safety switch. Ignition 'on', hand brake 'off', unscrew and lift filler cap 25 mm (1 in.); warning light should be illuminated

Check thickness of front brake pads, minimum 3 mm (0.125 in.), also check for oil contamination on brake pads and discs

Check and if necessary adjust rear wheel brakes. This automatically adjusts the hand brake

Change fluid in brake system every eighteen months

CONTINUED OVERLEAF

Wheels and tyres

Change round, wash and examine all road wheels for possible damage. Finally tighten all road wheel nuts

Check tyre pressures and inspect tyre treads and side walls for possible damage. Minimum tread depth 1 mm. Pressures: Front and rear: 1,8 kg/cm^2 (26 lb/sq in.), 1.79 bars

Propeller shaft

Lubricate sliding joint

Electrical

Check battery acid level and specific gravity of the electrolyte

Road test

Give car a thorough road test and carry out any adjustments required

Run car with reserve fuel control out for a short period to ensure that the control operates correctly. Push control in

Check operation of all lights

After test, check for oil, fuel, fluid or grease leaks at all plugs, flanges, joints and unions. Check all brake pipes and hoses for chafing or looseness

Report any defects

Cleaning

Wipe clean all controls, handles, etc., clean windscreen and lights

MAINTENANCE
ATTENTION AT
64.000 KM (40,000 MILES)

For recommended lubricants and capacities see Part Three of this book, pages 60 and 61

Owner's signature.. giving authority for the work detailed below to be carried out

**Carried out by
Rover Distributor or
Dealer**

NAME ....

ADDRESS ....

....

We certify that the 64.000 km
(40,000-mile) maintenance
attention has been completed

Signature...................................

Km..

Mileage......................... ..,................

Date ....

Engine

Note and report any oil leakage for rectification action
Drain and refill engine sump
Renew external oil filter element
Tune up engine as follows using electronic equipment
(a) Check dwell angle, 26°–28°
(b) Check ignition timing. Dynamic setting, 6° BTDC at 500–600 rpm
(c) Check carburetter slow-running ⎫ Engine at normal
(d) Check mixture setting   ⎭ running temperature
Check oil in carburetter hydraulic dampers
Replace air cleaner elements
Clean filter in automatic enrichment device
Replace fuel filter
Replace breather filter
Clean flame traps
Replace sparking plugs. Gap: 0,60 mm (0.025 in.)
Important—Use only Champion L87Y sparking plugs
Check distributor contact points. Dwell angle 26°—28°
Lubricate and clean distributor
Check water level in screen washer reservoir (add Isopropyl alcohol in winter)
Check water level in radiator (anti-freeze)
Check fan and power steering pump belts. Fan belt 11 to 14 mm (0.437 to 0.562 in.) and power steering belt 6 to 9 mm (0.25 to 0.375 in.) free movement when checked midway between pulleys

Automatic transmission

Note and report any oil leakage for rectification action
The automatic gearbox level should be checked with engine idling and 'Park' selected
Check fluid level, top-up if necessary to 'full' mark on dipstick

Check oil pressure in automatic transmission:
(a) Chock front wheels and apply handbrake firmly Apply foot brake during test
(b) Connect pressure gauge and tachometer
(c) Start the engine and allow to warm up
(d) Move selector lever to 'D' or '2' position. ('D2' or 'D1' on early models)
(e) The pressures should be:
At 1,000 rpm 90-105 lb/sq in. (6,3-7,3 kg/cm^2)
(f) If pressure is more than 105 lb/sq in. (7,3 kg/cm^2) screw in downshift cable adjuster

Rear axle

Note and report any oil leakage for rectification action
Drain and refill differential

Steering and suspension

Note and report any oil leakage for rectification action
Check fluid level in power steering reservoir, top-up if necessary to 'high' mark on dipstick
Check that rubber boots on steering ball joints and ball swivels are not dislodged or damaged
Check front hubs for leakage
Check front wheel alignment:
1,5 mm (0.062 in.) toe-in to 1,5 mm (0.062 in.) toe-out

CONTINUED OVERLEAF

Brakes. See also Road Test

Check fluid level in reservoir, top-up if necessary to rib on, filter. Use Girling Crimson Brake Fluid (Specification J. 1703)

Check operation of reservoir level safety switch. Ignition 'on' hand brake 'off', unscrew and lift filler cap 25 mm (1 in.); warning light should be illuminated

Check thickness of front brake pads, minimum, 3 mm (0.125 in.), also check for oil contamination on brake pads and discs

Check and if necessary adjust rear wheel brakes. This automatically adjusts the hand brake

Renew all rubber seals and fluid in brake system. This should be done every three years if mileage covered is less than 64.000 km (40,000 miles). Refill with correct fluid. Girling Crimson Brake Fluid (Specification J. 1703)

Replace brake servo filter
Change fluid in brake system every eighteen months

Wheels and tyres

Change round, wash and examine all road wheels for possible damage. Finally tighten all road wheel nuts

Check tyre pressures and inspect tyre treads and side walls for possible damage. Minimum tread depth 1 mm. Pressures: Front and rear: 1,8 kg/cm^2 (26 lb/sq in.), 1.79 bars

Propeller shaft

Lubricate sliding joint

Electrical

Check battery acid level and specific gravity of the electrolyte

Clean. grease and tighten battery terminals

Check headlamp and fog lamp beam setting

Oil can lubrication

Apply a few spots of oil to throttle linkage, hand brake linkage, door locks, etc.

Road test

Give car a thorough road test and carry out any adjustments required

Run car with reserve fuel control out for a short period to ensure that the control operates correctly. Push control in

Check operation of all lights and instruments

After test, check for oil, fuel, fluid or grease leaks at all plugs, flanges, joints and unions. Check all brake pipes and hoses for chafing or looseness

Report any defects

Cleaning

Wipe clean all controls, handles, etc., clean windscreen and lights

NOW THAT ALL THE VOUCHERS IN THIS BOOK HAVE BEEN COMPLETED YOU ARE STRONGLY ADVISED TO APPLY TO YOUR ROVER DISTRIBUTOR OR DEALER FOR A COPY OF THE CONTINUATION MAINTENANCE SCHEDULE BOOK TO ENABLE THE GOOD WORK OF PREVENTATIVE MAINTENANCE TO BE CONTINUED FOR ANOTHER **64.000 KM (40,000 MILES)**

Part No. 605215

Issued July 1967

3rd re-issue
May 1969

4th re-issue
October 1970

Rover 3 & 3.5 Litre
Workshop Manual
Saloon and Coupé

Part No. 4661 & 605368

3 LITRE   **3·5**

TWO

OTHER

BOOKS

FOR

ROVER

3

AND

3.5 LITRE

OWNERS

Rover 3 & 3.5 Litre
Parts Catalogue
Saloon and Coupé

Part No. 605204

3 LITRE   **3·5**

From Rover dealers or, in case of difficulty, direct from the distributors:

Brooklands Books Ltd., PO Box 146, Cobham, Surrey KT11 1LG, England. Phone: 01932 865051
Brooklands Books Ltd., 1/81 Darley St., PO Box 199, Mona Vale, NSW 2103, Australia. Phone: 2 9997 8428
CarTech, 11481 Kost Dam Road, North Branch, MN 55056, USA. Phone: 800 551 4754 & 612 583 3471

ISBN 1 85520 2948
Printed and issued in England by Brooklands Books Ltd.
PO Box 146, Cobham, Surrey, KT11 1LG, England
With the kind permission of Rover Group Limited
B-RV60HH